Around
the World in
80 Purees

Dedicated to Sunil, Kirina, Ela, and Jyoti
The four most important souls in my life

Text copyright © 2016 by Leena Saini
Photography copyright © 2016 by Christine Han

Library of Congress Cataloging in Publication Number: 2015957078

ISBN: 978-1-59474-895-0

Printed in China
Typeset in Butternut, Chronicle, Playfair Display, and Verlag

Designed by Andie Reid
Production management by John J. McGurk
Food styling by Yossy Arefi
Ceramic wares courtesy of Shino Takeda and Jessie Lazar

Quirk Books
215 Church Street
Philadelphia, PA 19106
quirkbooks.com

10 9 8 7 6 5 4 3 2 1

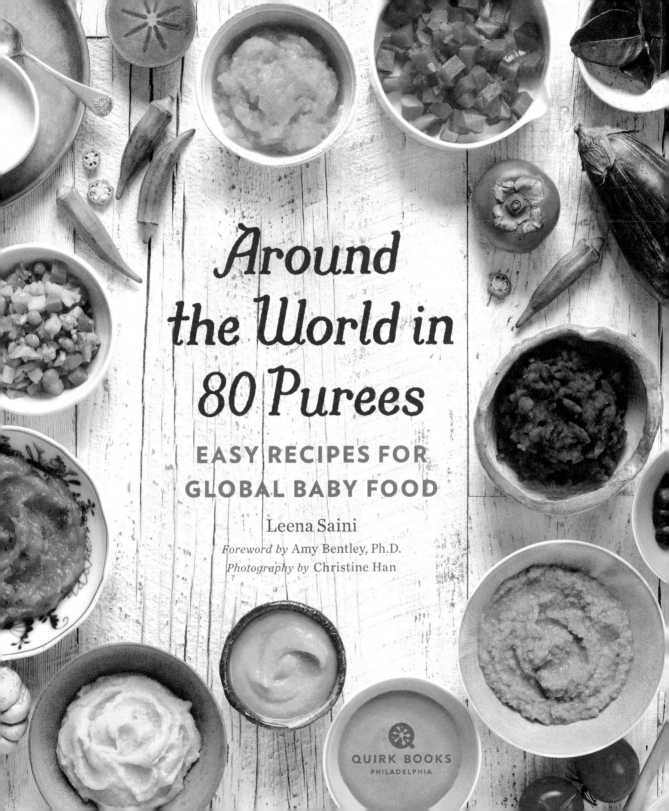

Around the World in 80 Purees

EASY RECIPES FOR GLOBAL BABY FOOD

Leena Saini

Foreword by Amy Bentley, Ph.D.
Photography by Christine Han

QUIRK BOOKS
PHILADELPHIA

Contents

A Whole Wide World of Purees

For Babies 6 Months and Up

A Spoonful of Flavor

For Babies 7-9 Months and Up

The Well-Seasoned High Chair

For Babies 10 Months and Up

Foreword

> *By Amy Bentley*

Across all societies, parents feed newborns with breast milk or a liquid equivalent at the beginning of the child's life, and at some point all move on to solid food. Between these phases is a transition period, known in the West as weaning, during which the frequency of breast- or bottle-feeding is gradually reduced and the ratio of liquid to solid food shifts. Cultures differ in beliefs about the appropriate age for introducing solids, as well as in their choice of first foods, which could include cereal, soup, congee, minced beef, camel butterfat, avocado, mashed beans, food first masticated by the parent, or a mixture containing the culture's signature combination of herbs and spices. Nearly all cultures, however, regard the transition to solids as significant. It is a moment that signals a decrease, albeit a limited one, in the child's dependence upon the parent and that signals a new period of exploration and interaction with the world.

In the United States we've begun to reexamine how we feed our babies: White rice cereal as a first food? Bland food rather than spiced meals? Introducing new foods slowly? Avoiding peanuts for as long as possible to stave off allergies? Recent research suggests that, in fact, the opposite of all these common practices is beneficial. Further, studies show that taste and smell are crucial to infant development even from the earliest moments.

As Americans have developed more cosmopolitan eating habits and culinary preferences, we've become aware that other cultures feed their infants differently, and it turns out that babies do just fine on curried rice and miso soup. In fact, as the recent spate of parenting books about France suggests, parents in other countries may be more successful at raising healthy, adventurous eaters. Creating a wide variety of globally inspired complementary foods for weaning infants not only is a question of taste, but may also be a question of optimal nutrition and health.

Leena Saini's amazing cookbook comes at exactly the right time. With *Around the World in 80 Purees*, you have the chance to explore a wide range of tastes and textures for your infant. Don't feel that you have to make baby food from scratch all the time. But when you do, let these recipes be a window into the marvelous, rich array of what "baby food" can be. Have fun exploring.

AMY BENTLEY, PH.D., is a professor in the Department of Nutrition and Food Studies at New York University. A food historian, she is the author of *Inventing Baby Food: Taste, Health, and the Industrialization of the American Diet* (University of California Press, 2014), which was a finalist for a James Beard Award. Learn more at inventingbabyfood.com.

Introduction

Introducing my daughter Kirina to solid food was one of the experiences of being a new parent that I looked forward to the most. The week her pediatrician gave my husband and me clearance to do so, we went straight to the grocery store and eagerly bought a box of organic baby rice cereal, just as the doctor recommended. We bought Kirina a special spoon, a cute pink bowl, and a bib. When we got home, I grabbed our best camera so I could catch the big cheeky smile she would certainly give us after her first bite. We prepared the cereal and fed her a spoonful.

She spit it out.

I was a little disappointed, but I knew this reaction was normal for a first solid meal. But on day 2 she spit out even more food. Days 3, 4, and 5 went the same way. Finally, to encourage her, I made a show of tasting the cereal—and nearly spat it out myself. Yuck! I wouldn't go near this bland, pasty mush. Why was I expecting her to eat it?

So the next day I mashed up an avocado and gave Kirina a taste. She gobbled it up.

Masala Baby

Helping my baby explore a world of flavors became my mission. I thought about the well-seasoned foods my husband and I eat and how I could make them baby-friendly. I scoured grocery store shelves for so-called ethnic baby food, but none existed. So I began to create my own flavorful baby food recipes.

At first, I used my childhood for inspiration, re-creating Indian meals my mom had made for me. I started by mashing dal (an Indian lentil dish) and then added the rice cereal that Kirina had previously rejected. Then I seasoned the mixture with one spice at a time, giving Kirina a chance to grow accustomed to one new flavor before introducing the next. I used this tactic for everything: Sweet potatoes with garam masala. Carrots with oregano for an Italian flair. A bit of cardamom in her applesauce or cinnamon in her pears. Over just a few weeks, Kirina learned to appreciate these new tastes.

She *was* a budding foodie after all!

Thinking outside the Jar

Next I began to research which foods babies around the world eat as their first meals. I interviewed mothers from different backgrounds; read cookbooks, history books, and international parenting books; even browsed baby food aisles of markets I visited abroad to see what they offered. What I discovered amazed me.

Indian babies eat all sorts of spiced lentils, rice, and curried vegetables as early as six months old. Japanese babies start with miso soup or broths flavored with seaweed, while Chinese babies feast on a rice porridge, known as congee, made with bits of mashed sweet potato or dried fish. Mexican babies are served fresh fruit with a dash of chili powder and a squeeze of lime. In fact, babies around the world usually eat what their parents are eating, only their servings are mashed or pureed. The texture might be different, but the seasonings and spices are the same—vibrant and appetizing. As a result, babies acclimate to their culture's tastes as soon as they are ready.

This book is for parents who are looking for ways to introduce their children to the flavors of the world, just as I was. Feeding little ones many foods early in life will help shape their palates and prepare them for enjoying a wider repertoire of foods and flavors as they age.

This book is also in honor of my mom, Dr. Jyoti D. Mankad, who inspired my love of cooking. She was one of the greatest women in the world, the best and most loving mother, and my best friend. Before she passed away in 2005, she had golden hands in the kitchen. She loved, loved, *loved* to cook, experiment with different flavors, and invent new dishes. I still miss her homemade dals, subjis, and rotis. Fortunately, she wrote down all of her recipes in a small notebook in the weeks before her death (still worried about feeding loved ones no matter the circumstance). My children will never be able to directly savor their grandmother's creative cooking. But I can share different flavors of the world with them, just as she did with me.

My goal is to inspire a love of world cuisine in Kirina, my younger daughter Ela, and all of your children as well. As a parent (or caregiver), you have an opportunity to expose your baby to diverse flavors. It is one of most lasting gifts you can give them.

From Kirina and Ela's highchairs to those of your own little ones, *bon appétit*!

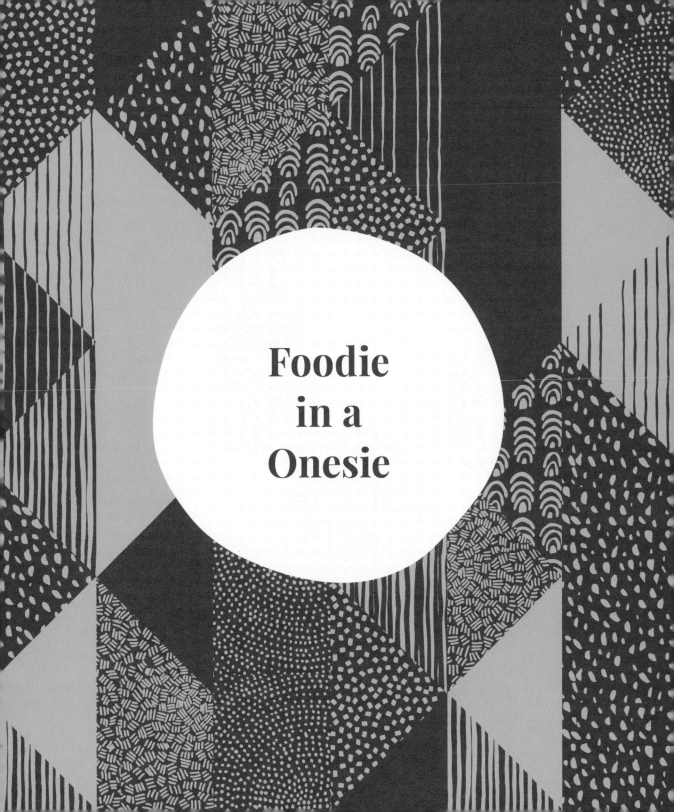

Foodie
in a
Onesie

Why Season Your Baby's Food?

Babies have from 2,000 to 10,000 taste buds. The best way to nurture flavor receptors is to expose them to different tastes as early as possible, which encourages babies to try new foods as they grow older. Studies have shown that babies who are exposed to a variety of tastes grow up to be more adventurous, less fussy eaters. This process begins earlier than you might think. Even while in utero, babies are able to taste what their mothers are eating via amniotic fluid. Breast milk also takes on flavors of the mother's daily diet, which in turn familiarizes the baby with new tastes. Over time, the herbs, spices, and other ingredients regularly offered to a child become part of that child's normal eating habits, increasing their likelihood of trying diverse foods.

Most babies in the United States are offered a limited range of bland foods. Dried, tasteless baby rice cereal, which is reconstituted with water or milk, is a common first food for a four-month-old. Next is jarred, watery, strained foods, such as peas or carrots, devoid of flavor; these are often oxidized into a dull, muddy color by the time they reach the jar. Depriving babies of fully flavored food can leave a lasting impact: Babies routinely exposed to monotonous, unseasoned dishes typically become conditioned to eat bland foods as they grow into toddlers and children.

In the United States parents often presume that children will have no interest in the offerings on the adult menu and that they'll naturally be picky eaters, shunning too-strong flavors or healthy ingredients. (Have you ever browsed the children's menu at a restaurant? Child meals are lumped into their own category where you will find macaroni and cheese, chicken nuggets, and french fries, regardless of the type of cuisine the restaurant serves.) The opposite is true in many other countries. In Japan, a child can be seen eating sushi with wasabi alongside their parents. In France, it's common to see children snacking on brie, water crackers, and onion quiche with their picnicking parents. Throughout several parts of the world, dining out of a jar or ordering off a "kiddie" menu is simply not an option.

So how can we tantalize our babies' taste buds like these parents around the globe? Start by spicing it up! Though it's true that we must be careful when introducing food to babies (see "Safe for Baby," page 17), it's almost impossible to start too early. Constant exposure is the only proven way to train tiny taste buds.

Baby-Friendly Spices

Remember that not all spices are spicy. In fact, a spice is just an aromatic ingredient used to season food—it can be hot and spicy, but it doesn't have to be.

"Baby-friendly" spices are those whose flavor is relatively mild, easy on new taste buds, and simple to digest. They are not short on flavor, just heat—think of spices such as cinnamon, saffron, cardamom, and clove. Baby-friendly savory spices, such as basil, coriander, cumin, and turmeric, pair well with vegetables and add depth to your little one's first bites.

Introducing seasoning is easy. When your baby becomes comfortable with a certain food—say, mashed banana or applesauce—kick it up a notch by adding a pinch of something from your spice cabinet. Start with ground cinnamon (one of the most baby-friendly spices, in my opinion) or a saffron thread. Over time, you can add multiple seasonings and different ingredients to broaden your baby's palate, working up to full-seasoned meals—even adding a tiny drop of hot sauce or vinegar, as fits the occasion. Try freshly squeezed lemon or lime juice in vegetable purees (also vary the vegetable—instead of carrots, try parsnips with dill; instead of spinach, try kale with garlic) or add a dash of fish sauce to soups and meats (think salmon with lemon, or chicken with coconut milk). Remember the flavors you enjoy and incorporate them into your baby's meals.

Just go slowly, adding one new flavor at a time, and don't give up if the first taste isn't a success. Parents commonly assume that if their baby spits out some food, she doesn't like it. That may not be the case. Your baby's taste buds are developing at their own pace, and they need practice to recognize and appreciate new flavors. Don't give up!

Safe for Baby

You're probably thinking, can I really put that in my baby's food? It's natural—and important—to want to make sure that every ingredient you feed your baby is safe and able to be easily digested. Adding herbs and spices to your baby's first bites is not only safe but also possibly beneficial. Turmeric has known antiseptic properties, and fennel is known to soothe an upset tummy. Even gripe water, a famous colic remedy, is made with dill, ginger, fennel, and chamomile. Let's not forget that parents around the world have been feeding their babies spices for centuries.

To safely introduce spices and herbs, follow these simple steps:

1. Listen to your baby's doctor. Most pediatricians recommend introducing herbs and spices after six months of age.

2. Treat each seasoning like a new food. After your baby's first taste of a new ingredient, wait to see if he is sensitive or allergic to it before cooking with it again.

3. Add just a pinch to start. A little goes a long way for tiny taste buds! Over time you can increase the amount, working up to fully seasoned meals.

4. Use baby-friendly spices (see opposite).

5. Always buy good-quality herbs and seasonings. Make sure spice blends aren't adulterated with preservatives or fillers.

6. Clean all ingredients appropriately before using them. Even if you peel something or discard the rind, wash it first. Bacteria can hide on the outside of fruits and vegetables and attach to your knife as you cut.

7. Taste the seasoned meal you plan to serve to make sure the flavor is not too strong. If you think the dish tastes good, chances are your baby will, too!

Passport to Flavor: Global Spices

It's a small world, and you'll find plenty of individual spices in a variety of cuisines. But some spices—and combinations—are flavorful postcards from particular regions or countries. Here are some to explore.

AFRICA	berbere • chili • cloves • coriander • cumin • fenugreek • garlic • ginger • grains of paradise • mint • pepper • sesame
CARIBBEAN	allspice • annatto • cinnamon • cloves • curry powder • ginger • Jamaican jerk spice • nutmeg • thyme
EASTERN EUROPE	caraway • cardamom • cloves • dill • horseradish • marjoram • mustard seed • paprika
EGYPT	aniseed • bay leaves • cardamom • cilantro • dill • dukkah • mint • parsley • saffron
FRANCE	bay leaf • garlic • herbes de Provence • nutmeg • parsley • sage • tarragon • thyme
GREECE	bay leaf • dill • fennel • Greek oregano • marjoram • parsley • tarragon • thyme
INDIA	asafetida • black mustard seed • cardamom • cloves • coriander • cumin • fennel • fenugreek • garam masala • garlic • ginger • saffron • turmeric
IRAQ/IRAN	cilantro • cinnamon • cumin • lime (dried) • mint • nutmeg • parsley • rose petals (dried) • saffron • sumac
ITALY	basil • garlic • marjoram • oregano • rosemary • thyme
JAPAN/CHINA/KOREA	chili • five-spice powder • garlic • ginger • scallion • sesame • soy • umeboshi • wasabi • yuzu

LEBANON	coriander • cumin • mint • thyme
MEDITERRANEAN	fennel • garlic • mastic • mint • oregano • rosemary • saffron • sage • thyme
MEXICO	allspice • annatto • chili • cilantro • cinnamon • cumin • oregano • vanilla
NORTH AFRICA/MOROCCO	cinnamon • cumin • dukka • ginger • harissa • orange blossom water • preserved lemon • ras el hanout • rose water • saffron
SCANDINAVIA	caraway • cardamom • cinnamon • dill • orange • parsley
SPAIN	coriander • fennel • paprika • parsley • saffron
SYRIA	allspice • cardamom • coriander • cumin • nutmeg • paprika • sumac
THAILAND/SOUTHEAST ASIA	chili • coriander • fish paste • galangal • garlic • ginger • makrut lime • lemongrass • lime • mint • sambal • shallot • tamarind • Thai holy basil • turmeric
TURKEY	cumin • mint • nigella • oregano • red pepper flakes • sumac

First Foods around the World

ALASKA/CANADA
seaweed and seal blubber

JAMAICA
cornmeal with
condensed milk

SWEDEN
välling (commercially
prepared wheat cereal
with palm oil and
powdered milk)

EGYPT
bread soaked
in milk

TIBET
tsampa (barley
flour mixed with
yak butter tea)

KOREA
rinsed kimchi

JAPAN
okayu (rice
porridge)
topped with
dried fish

NIGERIA
yam flour
porridge

INDIA
salty tea
boiled with
dried fruit

YUCATÁN
posole (soup
with hominy)

**DEMOCRATIC
REPUBLIC OF
THE CONGO**
bidia (cassava and
maize flour gruel)

INDONESIA
air tajin (rice
cooking water)

MEXICO
tortillas soaked in soup or
sweetened with vanilla; fruit
with chili powder and lime

VIETNAM
soup with fish
sauce, shrimp,
and pork bones

Equipment

You may already have everything you need to make baby food at home. The tools don't have to be fancy or designed specifically for making baby food; the most important thing is that you like them and are comfortable using them.

FOOD PROCESSOR OR BLENDER

The most essential tool you need is something to puree your baby's food. Several options exist, ranging from simple food mills to specialized baby-food makers. I use a mini food processor and an immersion blender, also known as a stick blender or hand blender. You also need a good spatula for scraping the sides of the food processor.

SAUCEPANS

I use thick stainless-steel pans because they prevent food from scorching. A 1-quart pan is great for steaming small quantities. A 2-quart pan is handy when cooking bulkier items like lentils or pasta or heating substantial quantities of liquid, so it won't boil over. A 6-quart pan is useful for boiling vegetables like potatoes. Pots with inserts or baskets are useful for steaming vegetables.

STORAGE CONTAINERS

Freezer-safe containers allow you to cook a dish once, freeze it in small portions, and then defrost whatever you need in a flash. I recommend 4- and 8-ounce glass containers or simply freezing purees in ice cube trays.

WOODEN SPOONS

Use them to mash lentils and grains of rice as they cook to create smoother porridges.

POTATO RICER

Although not essential, this gadget is great for pureeing a variety of fruits and vegetables, especially potatoes, which can become gummy when processed in other machines. The ricer keeps potatoes light and airy, creating a creamier, smoother mash, and ensures lump-free purees, which are especially good for younger babies.

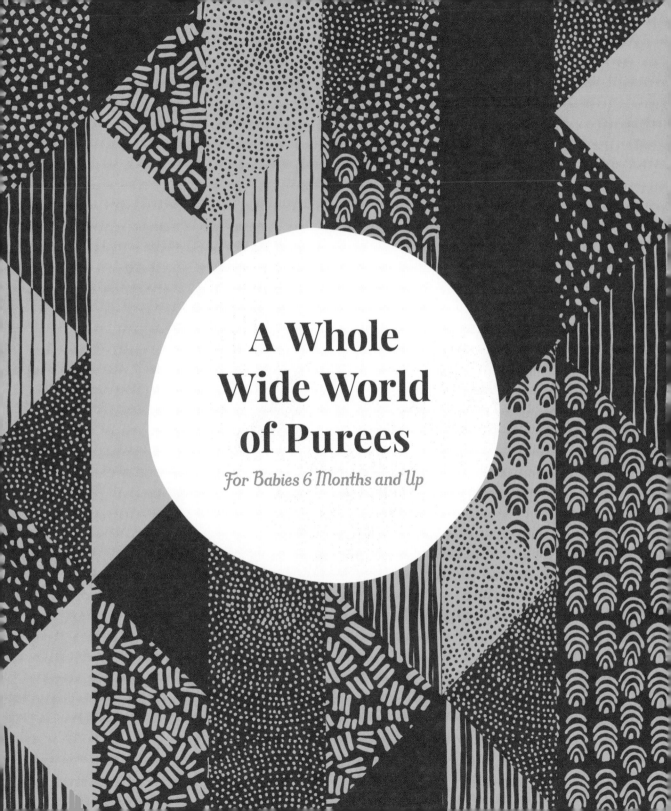

A Whole Wide World of Purees

For Babies 6 Months and Up

Mango Oatmeal

INDIA/CARIBBEAN MAKES ABOUT 16 OUNCES

Infant oatmeal flakes are a great invention for exhausted new parents. They're a quick and easy way to add more substance to simple fruit purees. But it's not too time-consuming to make home-made oatmeal instead. This version uses mango, the much-revered national fruit of India, Pakistan, and the Philippines.

A WORLD OF FLAVOR:
Mango

This sweet, fleshy fruit is high in vitamins A and C, potassium, and beta-carotene. Buy good-quality mangoes; they can be fibrous and displeasing to babies. They are typically in season from March through June.

3 tablespoons infant oatmeal cereal

2 ripe mangoes, or 2 cups frozen mango chunks

2 tablespoons (1 ounce) water, breast milk, formula, or whole milk

1–2 tablespoons plain whole milk yogurt, optional

PREP Prepare oatmeal according to package directions. Peel mangoes and cut into chunks; you should have 2 cups. (If using frozen fruit, allow to defrost.)

MAKE Place mangoes in a mini food processor and puree, adding liquids as necessary to blend. For younger babies, puree until smooth. Leave a bit chunkier for babies over 9 months old.

SERVE Transfer puree to a small bowl. Add oatmeal and yogurt (if using) and stir well to combine. Serve immediately.

Thanks to frozen chunks and purees, you can share fruits like guava (as well as papaya, mango, and more) with your little ones, too. Add a pinch of cinnamon or nutmeg for extra flavor.

Guava Oatmeal

CENTRAL AND SOUTH AMERICA MAKES ABOUT 8 OUNCES

2–3 tablespoons prepared infant oatmeal cereal

2–3 ripe guavas, peeled and cut into chunks

MAKE Puree guava in a mini food processor. Combine with oatmeal, stirring well.

SERVE Serve immediately.

Paired with mango and cinnamon, bananas are pleasingly intense yet mild enough for little ones, too.

>Variation

Spiced Mango Banana Oatmeal Add 1/8 teaspoon Spanish saffron threads, a pinch ground allspice, or a pinch ground cardamom while blending.

Mango Banana Oatmeal with Cinnamon

INDIA/CARIBBEAN MAKES ABOUT 16 OUNCES

2 mangoes, peeled and cut into chunks, or 2 cups frozen mango chunks, defrosted

1 large ripe banana, peeled and cut in half

Pinch ground cinnamon

2 tablespoons (1 ounce) water, breast milk, formula, or whole milk

3 tablespoons prepared infant oatmeal cereal

2–3 tablespoons plain whole milk yogurt, optional

MAKE Place mango, banana, and cinnamon in a mini food processor and puree, adding liquid as necessary to blend. For younger babies, puree until smooth. Leave mixture a little chunkier for babies older than 9 months.

SERVE Transfer mixture to a small bowl. Stir in oatmeal and yogurt (if using). Serve.

Pineapple Oatmeal

CARIBBEAN MAKES ABOUT 8 OUNCES

2–3 tablespoons infant oatmeal cereal

1 cup fresh pineapple chunks or 1 cup frozen pineapple chunks, defrosted

1 banana, peeled and cut in half

2 tablespoons (1 ounce) water, breast milk, formula, or whole milk

Sweet, juicy, vibrant pineapple is a most delicious introduction to tropical fruits. Banana helps bind the oatmeal, but you can omit it for purer pineapple flavor.

MAKE Prepare oatmeal according to package directions. Place pineapple, banana, and oatmeal in a mini food processor and puree, adding liquid as necessary to blend. For babies younger than 9 months, puree with a stick blender until smooth. Leave chunkier for babies over 9 months old.

SERVE Serve at room temperature.

Cardamom Pear Oatmeal

SCANDINAVIA MAKES ABOUT 16 OUNCES

2–3 tablespoons infant oatmeal cereal

4–5 Bartlett pears, sliced evenly (about 2 cups)

¼ teaspoon ground cinnamon

⅛ teaspoon ground cardamom

A pinch of spice combined with sweet fruit transforms oatmeal into something special. Cardamom, a popular ingredient in Scandinavian baking, pairs delightfully with sweet, fleshy, juicy fruits like pear. Perfectly ripe pears are best.

MAKE Prepare oatmeal according to package directions. In a 2-quart saucepan place pears, cinnamon, cardamom, and ¼ cup water. Simmer, covered, on medium-low heat for about 8 to 10 minutes, until soft. Let cool. Puree in mini food processor.

SERVE Mix oatmeal into puree. Serve immediately.

Cardamom Banana Oatmeal

INDIA MAKES ABOUT 8 OUNCES

2–3 tablespoons infant oatmeal cereal

1 ripe banana

2 tablespoons (1 ounce) breast milk, whole milk, or formula

1 tablespoon plain whole milk yogurt, optional

⅛ teaspoon ground cardamom

Cardamom is essential in Indian and Middle Eastern cooking. Its warm, inviting taste is accessible to babies, which makes it perfect for this recipe. This oatmeal is equally tasty warmed or chilled.

A WORLD OF FLAVOR:
Cardamom

Cardamom's spicy-sweet flavor is the key to chai tea. Its green pods contain little black seeds that are sold either whole or ground. Use it to season foods both sweet and savory.

PREP   Prepare oatmeal according to package directions. Peel banana and cut in half.

MAKE   Place banana and milk in a mini food processor and puree until smooth. Blend together, adding more milk if necessary to create a smooth puree.

SERVE   Transfer puree to a small bowl. Add oatmeal and yogurt (if using) and stir well to avoid lumps. Stir in cardamom and serve.

>Variation

Cardamom Mango Oatmeal Add 1 mango, peeled and chopped (about 1 cup), with or instead of banana.

Spiced Fruity Oatmeal

Experiment with fruits and spices to evoke different cuisines. Here are two to get you started.

German/Nordic flavors:
PEAR WITH GROUND NUTMEG, GROUND ALLSPICE, OR FRESHLY GRATED GINGER

Eastern European flavors:
APPLE WITH GROUND NUTMEG, CINNAMON, CARDAMOM, OR ALLSPICE

Mango Banana Saffron Oatmeal

INDIA MAKES ABOUT 10 OUNCES

For adults all over India, fresh chunks of mangoes and bananas seasoned with saffron make for a wonderful summer fruit salad. Its sweet, bright flavors also make for a tasty breakfast oatmeal.

Pinch Spanish saffron threads

1 tablespoon warm water

1 cup fresh, ripe, peeled mango chunks or 1 cup frozen mango chunks, defrosted

1 large ripe banana, peeled and sliced

3 tablespoons prepared infant oatmeal cereal

2–3 tablespoons whole milk plain yogurt, optional

PREP Soak saffron threads in warm water. Mash threads lightly with the back of a spoon until the color emerges.

MAKE Place saffron/water mixture, mango, and banana in a mini food processor. For babies younger than 9 months, puree until smooth. Leave chunkier for babies over 9 months old.

SERVE Stir in oatmeal cereal and yogurt (if using) and serve.

Masala Chai Oatmeal

INDIA MAKES ABOUT 2 OUNCES

4 tablespoons infant oatmeal cereal (or 4 tablespoons homemade oatmeal)

4 tablespoons breast milk, formula, whole milk, or plain whole milk yogurt

Pinch ground cinnamon

Pinch ground cardamom

Pinch ground ginger or grated fresh ginger

MAKE In a small bowl, prepare oatmeal with the liquid according to package directions. If using yogurt, add milk to thin to desired consistency.

SERVE Stir in cinnamon, cardamom, and ginger. Serve immediately.

Masala Chai Spice Blend

With a mortar and pestle or in a clean coffee grinder, grind into a fine powder 1 teaspoon whole cardamom seeds, a ½-inch piece of cinnamon stick or ½ teaspoon ground cinnamon, 10 whole cloves or ½ teaspoon ground cloves, 1 pinch freshly grated nutmeg, and ⅛ teaspoon ground ginger. Store in an airtight container. Add ¼ teaspoon or to taste to your baby's oatmeal—or to your own cup of tea. Makes about 2 teaspoons.

"My baby can't drink chai tea!" you say, and you're right. But she can have the same spices used to make it, and you can enjoy the flavors together. I like serving this oatmeal warm because the heat brings out the sweetness of the milk, which babies usually appreciate. But it is also delicious when chilled, though the flavors are slightly different.

A WORLD OF FLAVOR:
Masala Chai

Masala chai literally means tea (*chai*) blended with a mixture of spices (*masala*). This cherished beverage, drunk throughout the day in India, is typically made with black tea, milk, and spices including cinnamon, clove, cardamom, ginger, and black pepper.

Congee

CHINA MAKES ABOUT 4 CUPS

A warm rice porridge also known as *jook, xifan, jyu-bai-gayu,* or *okayu,* congee (pronounced "*kahn*-gee") is a traditional Asian breakfast and all-around comfort food that many Chinese, Malaysian, Japanese, and other Asian parents make as a first food for their babies. Even as early as four months old, babies are served the cooking water used to make this rice porridge for extra nutrition. Easy to digest, congee can be used as a vehicle to introduce other fruits, vegetables, and flavors to your baby's diet.

½ cup long-grain white rice

PREP Place rice in a 2-quart saucepan and wash with plenty of water. Using clean hands, swirl rice around in pot and scrub with fingers. When water turns cloudy, carefully pour it out and add fresh water, repeating several times until water is mostly clear. Drain and add 5 cups of fresh water.

MAKE Bring rice to a boil over medium-high heat. If froth appears, skim it off with a spoon. Cover, lower heat to a simmer, and cook for 25 to 30 minutes, until rice grains are soft. The consistency, especially for younger babies, should be smooth and porridgelike (on the thin side). Check pot frequently to make sure it doesn't boil over; keep lid ajar when necessary. Toward the end of cooking time, stir often with a wooden spoon to break up grains and prevent rice from sticking to the pan. Adjust cooking time as necessary.

SERVE Congee can be served warm or at room temperature.

>Variations

Sweet Potato Congee Peel 1 sweet potato and cut into 1-inch chunks. Bring a medium pot of water to a boil. Add potatoes and boil until soft. For younger babies, puree cooked potatoes with a little bit of the cooking water until smooth; leave some soft chunks for older babies. Stir potatoes into prepared congee.

Squash Congee Preheat oven to 400°F. Lightly grease a baking sheet with olive oil. Peel 1 butternut squash, acorn squash, pumpkin, or other squash. Cut into evenly sized chunks and arrange on baking sheet. Roast for about 30 minutes, until soft enough to mash with your fingers. *For babies younger than 9 months:* Puree about 1 cup roasted squash in a mini food processor or blender and add to prepared congee. *For babies over 9 months old:* Dice squash into small pieces and add to prepared congee.

Carrot and/or Pea Congee Boil 1 cup peeled and sliced fresh carrots or 1 cup frozen peas (or ½ cup of each) over medium-high heat until soft. *For babies younger than 9 months:* Puree and add to prepared congee. *For older babies:* Leave cooked vegetables as they are and add to prepared congee.

Mix-and-Match Congee

Once your baby is ready, start experimenting with congee. Try brown, basmati, and jasmine rice. Add different vegetables, meats, and seasonings (one at a time). Start with a pinch, drizzle, or drop of one of the following, and learn what your baby prefers. Feel free to mix and match!

BEAN CURD OR TOFU BITS

MINCED SCALLIONS

SOY OR FISH SAUCE

MINCED BOK CHOY

MINCED FRESH GINGER

NORI (TOASTED SEAWEED)

SHREDDED CHICKEN, PORK, OR BEEF

SESAME OIL

MASHED WHITE FISH

SAUTÉED GARLIC OR SHALLOTS

Taking its name from the Afrikaans word for "mealy porridge," *mieliepap* (pronounced "mee-lee-pap"), or pap, is a staple food of South Africa. Babies, children, and adults regularly eat this cornmeal porridge in various sweet and savory forms throughout the day.

Mieliepap

SOUTH AFRICA MAKES ABOUT 2 CUPS

2½ cups whole milk or water (or a combination)
¾ cup medium-grain stone-ground cornmeal
1 teaspoon unsalted butter, optional
½ teaspoon salt, optional

MAKE In a 2-quart saucepan over medium-low heat, bring milk to a boil. Slowly pour in cornmeal, stirring continuously. Lower heat to a simmer and cook uncovered for about 5 minutes, adding a little water if mixture becomes too thick.

SERVE Stir in butter and salt (if using). Serve warm.

Millet is a mildly flavored grain that's high in fiber and magnesium and easily digested. In Germany, millet porridge is a comforting breakfast food and a popular first cereal for babies. It is often served with cooked fruit, honey, and vanilla.

>Variation

Fruity Millet Porridge Add 1 teaspoon red currant, blackberry, or raspberry jam to porridge. Or try pureed figs, apricots, or dates.

Hansel and Gretel Porridge

GERMANY MAKES ABOUT 4 OUNCES

Pinch vanilla powder or seeds from a fresh vanilla bean pod
¾ cup whole milk
½ cup water
3 tablespoons whole millet
2 tablespoons applesauce
Drizzle honey, for babies over 12 months old

MAKE In a 2-quart saucepan over medium-low heat, bring vanilla, milk, and water to a boil. Add millet, cover, and simmer, adding water if mixture begins to dry out, for 20 to 30 minutes, until creamy. Toward the end of cooking, stir continuously with a wooden spoon.

SERVE Stir in applesauce. Drizzle with honey (if using). Serve warm.

Khichdi

INDIA MAKES ABOUT 8 OUNCES

½ cup dried split red lentils (masoor dal) or split green lentils (moong dal)

½ cup basmati rice

Pinch ground turmeric

½ teaspoon ghee or unsalted butter for serving, optional

Khichdi (pronounced *"kich*-dee") is a versatile Indian comfort food—a warm, inviting dish of creamy rice and softened lentils. It's easy to digest, high in protein and fiber, and simple to make. And it's among the first solid meals babies in India typically eat.

PREP Inspect lentils carefully, picking out sediment. Place lentils and rice in a 2-quart saucepan. Rinse thoroughly 3 or 4 times and drain.

MAKE Add turmeric and 2 cups water to pot. Cover and bring to a boil over high heat. Lower heat to medium-low and cook for 20 to 25 minutes, until mixture is soft and has the consistency of porridge (add additional water if too thick). Toward the end of cooking time, stir a few times with a wooden spoon to mash grains. Let cool for 5 minutes.

SERVE For babies younger than 9 months, puree with a stick blender; leave as is for older babies. Serve warm, topped with ghee (if using).

>Variations

Spiced Khichdi Add a pinch of garam masala and, if desired, salt to lentils before boiling.

Khichdi with Onion and Ginger In a pan over medium-low heat, sauté ¼ to ½ cup diced onion, ½ teaspoon minced garlic, and ½ teaspoon minced fresh ginger in 1 teaspoon ghee or olive oil for 5 to 7 minutes, until soft. Stir into prepared khichdi.

Khichdi with Vegetables Sauté ½ cup frozen vegetables, ¼ to ½ cup diced onion, ½ teaspoon minced garlic, and ½ teaspoon minced fresh ginger in 1 teaspoon ghee or olive oil for 5 to 7 minutes, until soft. Stir into prepared khichdi.

In Russia, millet porridge is typically made with milk, not water. This favorite Russian breakfast known as *kasha tykva* (pronounced "*kash*-ah *tick*-vah") combines millet with pumpkin and spices. It is said to warm the soul on a cold day.

Pumpkin Millet Porridge

RUSSIA MAKES ABOUT 4 OUNCES

1¼ cups whole milk

3 tablespoons whole millet

2 tablespoons pureed pumpkin

⅛ teaspoon ground cinnamon

⅛ teaspoon freshly grated nutmeg

About 1 teaspoon honey, for babies over 12 months old, optional

MAKE In a 2-quart saucepan, bring milk and millet to a boil over medium heat. Turn heat to low, cover, and let simmer for 25 minutes. Add pumpkin and cinnamon and cook, uncovered, over medium heat, stirring constantly for 7 to 10 minutes, until creamy. Let cool. Stir in nutmeg.

SERVE For babies over 12 months, drizzle with honey to taste (if using). Serve warm.

This applesauce will fill your entire home with the smell of warm cinnamon and saffron—a kind of aromatic hug. The saffron imparts a lovely blush color as well.

Saffron Applesauce

SPAIN MAKES ABOUT 1½ CUPS

5 red apples (Macintosh, Gala, Pink Lady and Cameo work well), peeled, cored, and sliced evenly

¼ teaspoon Spanish saffron threads

Pinch ground cinnamon

MAKE Place apples, ¼ cup water, saffron, and cinnamon in a 2-quart saucepan. Cover and cook over medium-low heat, stirring occasionally, for 10 to 15 minutes, until apples are soft. Let cool.

SERVE For babies younger than 9 months, puree in a mini food processor until smooth; leave as is for older babies. Serve warm.

SAFFRON
APPLESAUCE

Serve this sweet puree for breakfast, or freeze it into popsicles if your baby is teething. Add a squeeze of lime juice for extra tropical dazzle.

A WORLD OF FLAVOR:
Guava

Guava is a small round fruit that tastes like a cross between a pear and a strawberry. Look for it fresh or frozen.

Guava Applesauce

SOUTH AMERICA MAKES ABOUT 16 OUNCES

1 cup peeled ripe fresh guava chunks or defrosted frozen guava puree

1 cup applesauce

2–3 tablespoons prepared infant oatmeal cereal

MAKE Puree guava and applesauce in a mini food processor until smooth.

SERVE Transfer puree to a small bowl and stir in oatmeal. Mix well to avoid lumps. Serve at room temperature.

This spiced pear puree reminds me of French open-air markets stacked with sweetly smelling fruits. Cloves and cardamom are classic European flavors, and cinnamon (see the variation) pairs well with either or both.

>Variation

Cinnamon Pear Sauce Omit cardamom and cloves. Add ⅛ to ¼ teaspoon ground cinnamon to pears before cooking.

Pear Sauce

FRANCE MAKES ABOUT 16 OUNCES

5 ripe pears (Bartletts work well), peeled, cored, and sliced evenly

⅛ teaspoon ground cardamom

⅛ teaspoon ground cloves

MAKE In a 2-quart saucepan combine pears, ¼ cup water, and spices. Cook on medium-low heat until pears are soft, about 10 to 15 minutes. Stir occasionally. Remove from heat and let cool.

SERVE For babies younger than 9 months, puree in mini food processor until smooth. Leave chunkier for babies over 9 months old. Leave as is for toddlers to eat as finger food. Serve warm or chilled.

Mango Saffron Puree

INDIA MAKES ABOUT 16 OUNCES

Pinch Spanish saffron threads

1 tablespoon warm water

2 cups peeled ripe fresh mango chunks or defrosted frozen mango chunks

PREP   In a small bowl, soak saffron threads in warm water. Mash threads lightly with the back of a spoon until color emerges.

MAKE   Place mangoes and saffron mixture in a mini food processor and puree.

SERVE   Serve chilled or at room temperature.

I grew up on the common Indian flavor combination of saffron and mango. The saffron subtly enhances the mango, cutting through its intense sweetness.

A WORLD OF FLAVOR:
Saffron

Saffron is mild and a bit sweet, making it baby friendly, and its deep red hue infuses whatever you're cooking with gorgeous color. Buy good-quality saffron threads. Avoid products that say "ground saffron": they are often adulterated with fillers.

Gingered Plum Puree

CHINA MAKES ABOUT 8 OUNCES

4 ripe black or red plums

2 thin slices peeled fresh ginger

PREP   Wash, pit, and chop plums.

MAKE   In a 1-quart saucepan, place plums, ginger, and 1 tablespoon water. Simmer over low heat for 3 to 5 minutes.

SERVE   Puree in a mini food processor and serve.

Traditional Chinese ginger and plum sauce is often served as a dipping condiment or a barbecue sauce for duck or pork. This version for babies involves simply stewing the plums with a bit of ginger. If your baby doesn't slurp it up, sweeten it with a bit of demerara sugar, baby yogurt, or honey (for babies 12 months and older).

Kadu Borani

AFGHANISTAN MAKES ABOUT 4 CUPS

2 small sugar pumpkins (about 2 pounds)

1 teaspoon olive oil

1 Roma tomato, chopped

3 fresh mint leaves, chopped, or pinch dried mint

1–2 thin slices peeled fresh garlic

Pinch ground coriander

2 tablespoons plain whole-milk yogurt, for babies older than 8 months

Yogurt is a traditional Afghani condiment and ingredient, often made fresh at home every few days. It's used in *kadu borani* (pronounced "ka-*doo* bore-ah-*nee*"), a side dish made by frying pumpkin (*kadu*) with a sweet tomato sauce that is served topped with garlic-mint yogurt (*borani*). You can substitute any squash for the pumpkin, or use canned puree.

PREP Preheat oven to 350°F. Remove pumpkin stems. Cut pumpkins in half and use a spoon to scoop out seeds. Cut each piece in half again and place on a baking sheet. Bake for 45 to 50 minutes, until soft and fork-tender. Let cool and peel skin, which should come off easily. Puree pumpkin and a few teaspoons water in a mini food processor or blender.

MAKE In a 2-quart saucepan, heat oil over medium-low heat. Add tomatoes and sauté for about 5 minutes, until saucelike in consistency and beginning to turn dark red.

SERVE For babies younger than 8 months: Add pumpkin and mint to tomatoes and cook for an additional 1 to 2 minutes. Let mixture cool, then puree in a mini food processor. Serve at room temperature.

For babies 8 months and older: Add garlic and coriander to tomatoes. Sauté for 5 minutes, until mixture is reduced to a thick sauce. Add pumpkin puree and cook for an additional 1 to 2 minutes. Top with a dollop of yogurt and a pinch of mint. Serve warm.

Bananas with Cardamom

INDIA MAKES ABOUT 8 OUNCES

One of my earliest spice-related memories is of my mother slicing bananas, sprinkling ground cardamom on top, and serving it to me as a typical afterschool snack. These flavors work for babies, too. Experiment by adding a pinch of ground cinnamon, freshly grated nutmeg, or ground allspice instead of cardamom, and try it with roasted bananas (see variation). Roasting fruits and vegetables brings out a different—often sweeter—flavor. See what your little one thinks.

2 firm yellow bananas with minimal brown spots

⅛ teaspoon ground cardamom

PREP   Peel bananas and cut them in half.

MAKE   For babies younger than 9 months, puree bananas and cardamom together in a mini food processor. Mash with a fork to achieve a chunkier texture for babies over 9 months old.

SERVE   Serve slightly chilled or at room temperature.

>*Variation*

Roasted Bananas with Cardamom Preheat oven to 400°F. Slice 2 unpeeled bananas lengthwise and place cut side down on an aluminum-foil-lined baking sheet. Bake for 12 to 15 minutes, or until peels blacken and fruit begins to bubble out of peel. Remove from oven and let cool for 5 minutes. Carefully remove peels. *For babies younger than 9 months:* Add cooled bananas and cardamom to a mini food processor and puree until smooth. *For babies over 9 months old:* Mash bananas and cardamom together with a fork to achieve a chunkier texture. Serve warm.

Papaya and Banana with Cinnamon and Nutmeg

MEXICO MAKES ABOUT 16 OUNCES

2 cups peeled ripe papaya chunks

1 large ripe banana, peeled and cut in half

Pinch ground cinnamon

Pinch freshly grated nutmeg

Whole milk or water as needed

MAKE Place all ingredients in a mini food processor and puree until smooth. Add a little water or milk if necessary.

SERVE Transfer to a small bowl and serve chilled or at room temperature.

Papaya and banana are common first foods for babies in Mexico. In this puree they are combined with cinnamon and nutmeg, two spices often used in Mexican desserts. Make this snack a meal by adding 2 to 4 tablespoons prepared infant oatmeal cereal.

A WORLD OF FLAVOR:
Papaya

Papaya, also known as pawpaw, is an oblong fruit native to southern Mexico and Central America with skin that changes from green to orange as it ripens, black seeds, and either yellow-orange or red flesh. It's also found in the Caribbean, Thailand, and Southeast Asian countries, where it's eaten raw or cooked. Ripe papayas are soft and sweetly fragrant.

Mangú

DOMINICAN REPUBLIC MAKES ABOUT 1 CUP

For two of the five years I lived in New York City, I was around the corner from Malecon Restaurant, which is well known for its authentic Latin American cooking. My favorite was their *mangú* (pronounced "mahn-*goo*"), a dish of mashed plantains topped with sautéed onions that originated in the Dominican Republic. Children were always eating this in the restaurant when I was there. As your baby gets older, top this dish with scrambled eggs or cheese for a filling meal.

A WORLD OF FLAVOR:
Plantains

Plantains are a large, firm variety of banana popular in parts of Latin America, Africa, and Asia. They are a great canvas for new flavors: try them with sautéed garlic or even just a couple pinches of salt and pepper. Boiling time will vary with ripeness. The riper the plantain, the faster it will cook.

1 unripe (green) plantain
Pinch ground cinnamon or allspice
½ teaspoon olive oil
¼ cup sliced red onions
Splash apple cider vinegar
Pinch salt, optional

PREP Peel plantain and cut into 1-inch slices.

MAKE In a 1-quart saucepan, combine 1½ cups water, plantains, and cinnamon. Bring to a boil over medium-high heat. Cover, reduce heat to medium-low, and boil gently for 10 to 15 minutes, until plantains are soft.

Meanwhile, in another saucepan, heat olive oil over medium heat. Add onions and sauté until light brown. Add a few teaspoons of water if they start to stick to the pan. Add vinegar and cook for 1 additional minute. Let cool. Drain plantains, reserving liquid. Return plantains to pot.

SERVE With a potato masher or fork, mash plaintains, adding cooking liquid as necessary to achieve a smooth consistency. Add salt (if using). Top with onions. For babies younger than 9 months, puree in a mini food processor until smooth. Leave as is for older babies. Serve warm.

Strawberry Basil Puree

FRANCE/ITALY MAKE ABOUT 4 OUNCES

1 cup fresh or frozen strawberries
2 fresh basil leaves

PREP Wash berries and trim the tops. Wash basil.

MAKE Puree strawberries and basil in a mini food processor.

SERVE Serve chilled or at room temperature.

This summery puree is inspired by Nice, France. The sun-kissed region is close to Italy, so the cuisine features the best flavors of both countries—not to mention the Provençal style of cooking, using fresh fruits, vegetables, and herbs from the nearby countryside. Strawberry and basil are a fresh combination your baby will love. And definitely make a little extra for yourself—it's incredible on a scoop of vanilla ice cream.

Strawberry Lychee Puree

CHINA MAKES ABOUT 8 OUNCES

1 cup fresh or frozen strawberries
4 fresh lychees or 4 canned lychees, rinsed

PREP Wash and trim berries.

MAKE Puree strawberries and lychees in a mini food processor.

SERVE Serve chilled.

Sweet, slightly tart, and with similar flavors, lychees and strawberries are an inspired match.

A WORLD OF FLAVOR:
Lychee

Sweet lychees (pronounced "*lee-chees*") are grown and consumed all over Southeast Asia. Their aroma is sweet, floral, and distinctive. Fresh lychees are best, but canned ones are more readily available. Just make sure to rinse off the syrup very well.

Mango with Coconut and Lime

MEXICO MAKES ABOUT 12 OUNCES

Coconut gives this tropical puree a smooth, creamy texture while mango and lime add both sweet and sour notes. Babies in Mexico are exposed to these flavors early in life. Here's a great way to introduce them to your baby, too.

2 cups ripe, peeled fresh mango chunks or defrosted frozen mango chunks

2 tablespoons coconut milk

1 to 2 tablespoons freshly squeezed lime juice

MAKE Puree all of the ingredients in a mini food processor.

SERVE Serve chilled.

Figs and Apricots with Aniseed

MOROCCO MAKES ABOUT ½ CUP

3 fresh or dried figs, cut in half

2 fresh apricots, washed and chopped (about 1 cup)

⅛ teaspoon ground aniseed

PREP If using dried figs, soak in water for 2 to 4 hours, until plump. Cut figs into small dice.

MAKE In a 1-quart saucepan, place figs, apricots, and aniseed. Add 2 tablespoons water, place pot over medium-low heat, cover, and steam for 3 to 4 minutes.

SERVE Puree mixture in a mini food processor, adding water as necessary to achieve a smooth consistency, and serve.

>Variation

Figs and Apples with Aniseed Omit apricots. Peel, core, and thinly slice 1 apple. Cook with figs, aniseed, and 2 tablespoons water for about 7 minutes, or until soft. Puree as directed above.

The fig tree is deeply rooted in history. It's been cultivated all over Asia since ancient times, and its fruit is mentioned in the Bible. The anise plant, native to many of the same regions as figs, is used to season a variety of foods, from breads to fruits to meats. It provides a licorice flavor to this unexpected puree. The apricots provide just a touch of tartness that balances the figs' sweetness.

A WORLD OF FLAVOR:
Figs

Today there are more than 700 varieties of figs, the most popular of which include purple-black Missions, yellow-green Kadotas, and green Calimyrnas. Fresh figs are plump, juicy, and very tasty. If you can find them, please feed them to your little one. Their growing season is short (typically June through October, depending on the variety), but dried figs are around all year and available without sulfites (a preservative). Organic, preservative-free varieties that are hydrated and ready to use are particularly convenient.

Cantaloupe with Cardamom

INDIA/CARIBBEAN MAKES ABOUT 4 CUPS

This comforting classic is one my mother used to make. Cool and refreshing, it was a nice contrast to all the spicy dishes on our summer dinner table. My favorite part was—and still is—the spice-infused juice that collects at the bottom of the bowl. *Note:* Don't forget to scrub the outside of the cantaloupe before you cut into it.

Fruit of ½ ripe cantaloupe, minced
⅛ teaspoon ground cardamom
Pinch granulated sugar, optional

MAKE For babies younger than 9 months, puree cantaloupe and cardamom in a mini food processor. For older babies, place minced melon in a glass or ceramic bowl and stir in cardamom.

SERVE Refrigerate for at least 30 minutes. Serve chilled.

Peaches with Basil

MEDITERRANEAN MAKES ABOUT 1 CUP

This recipe couldn't be simpler to make or more refreshing to eat. The basil-peach flavor combination is common in Mediterranean cuisine, but you won't find this tasty blend in a jar.

2 ripe peaches
3 fresh basil leaves

PREP Bring a large pot of water to a boil over high heat. Add peaches and boil uncovered for about 1 minute. Remove peaches with tongs and let cool. Once cool, use your fingers to remove skins; they should come off easily.

MAKE Halve peaches, remove pits, and chop coarsely. Place peaches and basil in a mini food processor and puree.

SERVE Serve chilled or at room temperature.

CANTALOUPE
WITH
CARDAMOM

Watermelon with Mint

IRAQ MAKES ABOUT 12 OUNCES

Mint is a staple herb in many places, including Iraq, Southeast Asia, Turkey, and Greece. It's used in everything from cucumber salad to tabbouleh to herbal tea.

2 cups chopped watermelon

1–2 fresh mint leaves

MAKE For babies younger than 9 months, puree watermelon and mint together in a mini food processor. For babies over 9 months old, dice watermelon into bite-size pieces and sprinkle with finely chopped mint.

SERVE Serve chilled.

Nashi Pear with Vanilla and Star Anise

JAPAN MAKES ABOUT 8 OUNCES

Crisp like an apple and juicy as a ripe pear, the Nashi pear, or Asian pear, is refreshing and indescribably tasty. Vanilla and star anise enhance the fruit's natural sweetness and tempt tiny taste buds.

2 Nashi pears, peeled and chopped (2 cups)

1 whole star anise

Pinch vanilla powder

MAKE In a 2-quart saucepan, place pears, star anise, vanilla powder, and 2 tablespoons water. Cover and simmer over medium heat for 7 to 10 minutes. Remove star anise and let cool for 5 minutes.

SERVE Puree in a mini food processor. Serve warm.

Mashed Cassava

SOUTH AMERICA MAKES ABOUT 1½ CUPS

1 pound fresh or frozen cassava, peeled and chopped

Pinch grated nutmeg

1 teaspoon butter, optional

Cassava is incredibly versatile. You can bake it, boil it, fry it, turn it into flour, or mash it. Start with this recipe featuring nutmeg, and then try whatever seasonings you like.

MAKE Place cassava in a 3-quart saucepan with enough water to cover it by about an inch. Boil, lid slightly ajar, over medium heat for about 25 to 30 minutes, until fork-tender. Drain, reserving cooking water.

SERVE Add nutmeg and butter (if using). Mash in pot with a little cooking water or puree in a mini food processor until smooth. Serve.

A WORLD OF FLAVOR:
Cassava

This sweet, starchy root vegetable, also known as yuca or manioc, can grow in near-drought conditions, gets high yields, and is a staple food. Mashed, it's a popular first food in South America, the Caribbean, and Africa.

Pineapple with Cinnamon Cream

CARIBBEAN MAKES ABOUT 12 OUNCES

1 ripe banana, peeled and cut in half

1 cup fresh or defrosted frozen pineapple chunks

¼ cup coconut milk or ½ cup coconut yogurt

⅛ teaspoon ground cinnamon

Water or whole milk for blending

Babies in tropical countries are introduced to coconut as early as six to eight months old. Coconut milk is a great way to start bringing this rich, sweet flavor into your baby's diet. Pineapple and cinnamon are natural pairings.

MAKE In a mini food processor, puree banana, pineapple, coconut milk, and cinnamon, adding water or milk to thin as necessary.

SERVE Serve chilled or at room temperature.

Cinnamon Coconut Curry

THAILAND/MALAYSIA/SOUTHERN INDIA MAKES ABOUT 1 CUP

½ cup coconut milk

1½ cups no-sodium chicken broth or water

Pinch ground turmeric

Pinch ground cinnamon

Pinch Spanish saffron threads, optional

1 cup frozen mixed vegetables

½ cup diced cooked chicken, optional

This is a fast and flavorful curry. The saffron lends a lovely fragrance and ochre color but can be omitted if you don't have it. For a heartier curry, add ½ cup cooked diced potatoes.

MAKE   In a 1-quart saucepan, place coconut milk, chicken broth, turmeric, cinnamon, and saffron (if using). Bring to a slow boil over medium heat. Add vegetables and cooked chicken (if using) and lower heat to maintain a simmer. Cook for 5 to 7 minutes, until vegetables are cooked and flavors have come together. Let cool for 5 minutes.

SERVE   For babies younger than 9 months, puree in a mini food processor. Leave as is for babies over 9 months old. Serve warm with fragrant white or brown jasmine or basmati rice.

Essentially a spinach curry, *saag masala* (pronounced "sahg ma-sa-la") is popular in northern India and typically mixed with mustard greens and paneer (fresh Indian cheese).

Saag Masala

INDIA MAKES ABOUT 2 CUPS

1 10-ounce bag baby spinach

1 teaspoon olive oil

⅛ teaspoon freshly grated ginger

Pinch garam masala

Pinch salt

MAKE In a large sauté pan over medium heat, warm 3 tablespoons water until steaming. Add spinach and cook, stirring frequently, for 3 to 4 minutes, until wilted. Let cool for 5 minutes. Place cooked spinach and liquid in a mini food processor. Puree, adding water as necessary.

Wipe sauté pan dry, add oil, and place over medium heat. Add ginger and cook for a few seconds. Add pureed spinach, garam masala, and salt. Cook for 1 to 3 minutes.

SERVE Serve warm or at room temperature.

>Variation

Spicier Saag Masala In a sauté pan over medium-high heat, warm 1½ teaspoons olive oil. Add ⅛ teaspoon whole cumin seeds and cook until they sputter. Add ⅓ cup chopped onions and lower heat to medium. Cook onions for 7 to 10 minutes, until light brown. Add spinach, ginger, garam masala, and salt. Cook for 3 to 4 minutes, until spinach is wilted. Let cool for 5 minutes. Puree in a mini food processor.

Sweet Aloo Gobi

INDIA MAKES ABOUT 2 CUPS

1 cup washed, peeled, and diced sweet potato

⅛ teaspoon freshly grated ginger

2 cups chopped cauliflower

Pinch ground cinnamon

Pinch garam masala

Aloo gobi (pronounced "ah-loo *go*-bee") is a typical North Indian curry, seasoned with a combination of spices called a masala, which includes black mustard seeds, cumin seeds, ginger, turmeric, and coriander. This baby-friendly version features sweet potatoes and ground cinnamon in order to appeal to little ones, who often appreciate sweetness in food.

MAKE   Place sweet potatoes and ginger in a 1-quart saucepan. Add just enough water to cover potatoes and bring to a boil over high heat. Lower heat to a simmer, cover, and steam for about 7 minutes, until soft. Transfer potatoes to a mini food processor; set aside. Add cauliflower to water and return to a boil. Lower heat, cover, and steam for 7 to 10 minutes, until soft. Transfer cauliflower to mini food processor. Reserve cooking water.

SERVE   Add cinnamon and garam masala to mini food processor and puree. Use some of the reserved cooking water as necessary to achieve a smooth consistency. Serve warm or at room temperature.

Mixed Vegetable Curry

SOUTHEAST ASIA MAKES ABOUT 2 CUPS

Consider this recipe more a suggestion than a formula. You can add whatever vegetables you have on hand and experiment with spice combinations. Add a few teaspoons of coconut milk in the last few minutes of cooking for a Thai- or Malaysian-style curry. Add shredded coconut for South Indian flair. And try it mixed with a little yogurt, as is typical in parts of India, Pakistan, and Malaysia.

½ cup washed, peeled, and diced russet potato

½ cup frozen diced carrots

½ cup frozen peas

½ cup chopped cauliflower

1 tablespoon olive oil

⅛ teaspoon black mustard and/or cumin seeds

¼ cup diced onions

1 Roma tomato, diced

Pinch turmeric

Pinch garam masala

Pinch salt

Plain whole-milk yogurt for serving

MAKE In a 2-quart saucepan, place vegetables and just enough water to cover them. Bring to a boil over high heat, then turn heat to low. Cover and simmer for 5 to 7 minutes, until vegetables are soft. Drain and set aside.

In another 2-quart saucepan, heat oil over medium-high heat. Add black mustard and/or cumin seeds and cook until they sputter, and then add onions. Lower heat to medium and cook for 5 to 7 minutes, or until onions begin to brown. Add tomatoes, turmeric, garam masala, and salt. Cook, stirring, for 3 to 5 minutes, until mixture resembles a sauce. Add vegetables and cook for another 3 minutes so flavors meld together. Let cool.

SERVE For babies younger than 9 months, mash with a potato masher or puree in a mini food processor, adding a bit of water as necessary. Leave as is for babies over 9 months old. Mix in about 1 teaspoon yogurt per serving.

India, Burma, and Nepal all have versions of this curry. Omit the onion for very young babies. For a Malaysian spin, add 2 to 3 teaspoons of coconut milk while sautéing the tomatoes.

Pea and Tomato Curry

INDIA MAKES ABOUT 2 CUPS

1 teaspoon olive oil

⅛ teaspoon black mustard seeds and/or cumin seeds

¼ cup diced onion, optional

2 Roma tomatoes, chopped

⅓ cup fresh or frozen sweet peas

⅛ teaspoon ground turmeric

Pinch salt

Pinch ground cumin and/or ground coriander

MAKE In a 1-quart saucepan, heat oil over medium-high heat. Add mustard seeds and cook until they sputter. Add onions (if using) and sauté until golden brown. Add tomatoes. Sauté over medium heat for 4 minutes. Add peas, turmeric, and salt. Stir for 4 minutes. Stir in cumin. Cook for 1 to 2 minutes.

SERVE Let cool for 5 minutes. Puree in a mini food processor. Serve.

Butternut squash puree is easy to dress up with sage, cinnamon, nutmeg, black pepper, or a pinch of any spice blend—try bharat from the Middle East, herbes de Provence from France, or ras el hanout from Morocco.

Curried Butternut Squash

INDIA MAKES 2 TO 4 CUPS

1 butternut squash, peeled and chopped

1 teaspoon curry powder

1 pat butter, optional

1 cup no-sodium chicken or vegetable broth

MAKE In a large pot over medium-high heat, boil squash for about 15 minutes. Drain. Add curry powder and butter (if using).

SERVE Puree in a mini food processor. Serve warm.

Baingan Bharta

INDIA MAKES ABOUT 2 CUPS

2 large eggplants

1½ tablespoons olive or vegetable oil

⅛ teaspoon cumin seeds

1 Roma tomato, chopped

¼ cup diced onion

⅛ teaspoon freshly grated ginger

⅛ teaspoon minced garlic

Pinch ground turmeric

Pinch garam masala

Pinch salt, optional

Lovingly prepared eggplant dishes are common kids' fare around the world, from India to Lebanon to the Mediterranean. But eggplant baby food is uncommon in the United States. This mildly spiced version of the northern Indian dish *baingan bharta* (pronounced "*bane*-gun burr-*tha*") is ideal for babies.

PREP   Preheat oven to 450°F. Place eggplants on a lightly greased rimmed baking sheet and bake for 45 minutes or until they collapse, flipping every 15 minutes to ensure even roasting. Transfer to a bowl and cover with plastic wrap. Let cool for at least 10 minutes. The steam will make the skin easier to remove. Once cool, chop off stems and remove as much skin as possible. Dice eggplant into small pieces, or process in a mini food processor. Set aside.

MAKE   In a 2-quart saucepan, heat oil over medium heat for 2 minutes. Add cumin seeds and cook until they sputter. Add tomatoes, onions, ginger, garlic, and turmeric. Cook for 5 to 7 minutes, or until onions are soft and slightly brown. Add eggplant and garam masala. Cook for 3 to 5 minutes.

SERVE   Puree in a mini food processor until smooth. Serve warm or at room temperature.

Avocado with Cilantro and Lime

MEXICO MAKES ABOUT 4 OUNCES

1 ripe avocado

1 teaspoon freshly squeezed lime juice

1 teaspoon washed and minced cilantro leaves

½ teaspoon ground cumin

PREP   With a sharp knife, cut avocado in half. Press the knife blade into the pit until firmly in place and then twist gently. The pit should pop out. Scoop out the flesh with a spoon.

MAKE   In a small bowl, combine all of the ingredients and mash together with a fork or wooden spoon.

SERVE   For babies younger than 9 months old, puree in a mini food processor until smooth. Leave chunkier for babies over 9 months old.

>Variation

Baby Guacamole In a small bowl, mash avocado flesh, 1 to 2 teaspoons tomato puree, a pinch of ground cumin, a squeeze of lime, and 2 or 3 minced cilantro leaves. *For babies younger than 9 months:* Add a little water as necessary to thin mixture. *For older babies:* Leave as is. As your baby becomes accustomed to these flavors, increase seasonings and add minced onion and a pinch of red chili powder. Soon you'll have worked your way up to fully seasoned grown-up guacamole.

In Mexico, babies eat their avocados sprinkled with chili and lime. The creamy, smooth flesh of this fruit is a versatile base for many Mexican, Caribbean, and South American seasonings. Try one with a pinch of ground coriander or even a pinch of chili powder. This version is a bright, citrusy homage to Mexican flavors that your little one will love.

A WORLD OF FLAVOR:
Cilantro

Cilantro, the Spanish word for coriander, refers to the fresh leaves and stems of the coriander plant. Mexican dishes rely heavily on this citrusy, pungent herb, and its flavor is one that babies there readily enjoy.

Italian-Style Carrots

ITALY MAKES ABOUT 6 OUNCES

Basil and oregano are used in countless Italian dishes, from pasta sauces to meats, and their delicate flavors make them good introductory herbs for babies. Caramelizing the onion brings out the vegetable's natural sugars, making it palatable to babies.

1 cup peeled, sliced carrots

1 cup no-sodium chicken broth or water

1 teaspoon olive oil

¼ cup diced yellow onion

Pinch salt

½ teaspoon minced garlic

1 Roma tomato, finely chopped

Pinch dried oregano, basil, or both

PREP In a 2-quart saucepan over medium-high heat, bring carrots and broth to a boil. Lower heat, cover, and cook for 5 to 7 minutes, until carrots are tender. Drain, reserving liquid. Set aside.

MAKE In a sauté pan, heat oil over low heat. Add onions and salt and sauté for 10 to 15 minutes, until light brown and caramelized. Add garlic and cook for 30 seconds. Add carrots, tomatoes, and oregano. Cover and cook for an additional 5 minutes, adding some reserved cooking liquid if mixture looks dry. Let cool for 5 minutes.

SERVE For babies younger than 9 months, puree in a mini food processor with additional cooking liquid as necessary. Leave as is for babies over 9 months old.

Oven-Roasted Carrots with Cumin

MOROCCO/NORTHERN AFRICA MAKES ABOUT 8 OUNCES

5 carrots

1 teaspoon olive oil

Pinch salt

¼ teaspoon ground cumin

Varying cooking techniques—steaming, roasting, braising, etc.—is another way to bring diversity to your baby's meals. Using a different technique can dramatically change the taste of a particular food. Roasting carrots, as here, enhances the vegetable's natural sweetness, and a bit of ground cumin adds a taste of Morocco.

PREP Preheat oven to 425°F. Wash carrots, trim tops, and peel them. Cut each in half horizontally. Then cut any thick pieces lengthwise, if necessary, so that all pieces are of equal thickness.

MAKE In a small bowl, toss carrots with olive oil and salt. Transfer to a baking sheet or roasting pan and bake for 15 minutes. Flip carrots and roast for an additional 15 minutes, until they have shrunk and are soft. Transfer carrots to a heatproof bowl. Add ground cumin and toss.

SERVE For babies younger than 9 months, puree with a stick blender and a little water as necessary. Cut into bite-size pieces for babies over 9 months old.

>Variation

Lemon Roasted Carrots Try a squeeze of lemon or orange juice along with or instead of the cumin. Or substitute oregano, coriander, ras el hanout, or curry powder for the cumin.

This nutritious puree is based on a Moroccan recipe for seasoning carrots with ginger, brown sugar, and dates. This baby version omits the sugar, but carrots and dates bring plenty of sweetness and flavor.

>Variation

Moroccan Carrots Try adding a pinch of ground turmeric, cumin, coriander, or grated orange zest during cooking.

Carrots with Dates and Ginger

MOROCCO MAKES ABOUT 8 OUNCES

1 cup carrots (about 2 carrots), peeled and diced or thinly sliced

¼ cup sulfite-free dried dates, pitted and chopped

2 thin slices fresh ginger

MAKE In a 1-quart saucepan, bring ½ cup water to a boil over medium-high heat. Add carrots, dates, and ginger. Cover, lower heat, and simmer for 10 to 15 minutes, until carrots are soft. Using a slotted spoon, transfer carrots and dates to a mini food processor. Reserve water.

SERVE Puree, adding cooking water as necessary. Serve. warm or at room temperature.

Gajar sabzi (pronounced "ga-*jur* sub-*gee*") might be the best way to eat carrots. At least I thought so as a child! My mother would set aside a portion for me before adding lots of fiery green chilies for the adults.

Gajar Sabzi

INDIA MAKES ABOUT 1½ CUPS

1 teaspoon vegetable oil

¼ teaspoon black mustard seeds

¼ cup diced onions, optional

2 cups shredded carrots

Pinch salt, optional

MAKE In a 2-quart saucepan, heat oil over medium-high heat. Add black mustard seeds and cook until they sputter. Add onions (if using) and cook for about 2 minutes, until translucent. Add carrots, salt, and ¼ cup water and lower heat. Cover and simmer for 5 to 7 minutes, or until carrots are soft. Add a little more water if mixture begins to dry out.

SERVE Puree in a mini food processor until smooth.

Neeps and Tatties

SCOTLAND MAKES ABOUT 16 OUNCES

2 cups peeled and chopped rutabaga (about 2 rutabagas)

1 cup peeled and chopped russet potato (about 1 large potato)

1 tablespoon unsalted butter

Whole milk, as needed

1 tablespoon chopped fresh parsley

Salt and pepper to taste

The national dish of Scotland, haggis (a pudding made with the liver, heart, and lungs of a sheep) is traditionally served with neeps and tatties (mashed rutabagas and potatoes). Yes, Scottish babies have tried it! Be sure to wash the potatoes before peeling them. For the smoothest consistency, use a potato ricer to puree the vegetables.

MAKE In a 2-quart saucepan, boil rutabagas over high heat for 15 to 20 minutes, until soft. Use a slotted spoon to transfer rutabagas to a bowl and set aside. Return water to a boil and add potatoes. Boil for 10 to 15 minutes, until soft. Drain water and add potatoes to bowl with rutabagas.

SERVE Press vegetables through a potato ricer or mash with a fork, adding butter and milk as necessary to create a creamy consistency. Stir in chopped parsley and salt and pepper to taste.

Island Sweet Potatoes

CARIBBEAN MAKES ABOUT 5 OUNCES

Allspice berries look like a pepper-corn but in fact taste like nutmeg, cinnamon, and cloves mixed together (that's why Europeans called it allspice when they first encountered it in Jamaica). Allspice takes center stage in Caribbean cooking and is one of the main spices used in Jamaican jerk seasoning. It adds a taste of the islands to this sweet potato and fresh ginger dish.

1 large sweet potato
1–2 thin slices peeled fresh ginger
Pinch ground allspice

PREP Peel and dice sweet potato. You should have 1 cup.

MAKE In a 2-quart saucepan, place potatoes, ginger, and just enough water to cover (about 1 cup). Bring to a boil over high heat. Cover, reduce heat to medium-low, and cook for 12 to 15 minutes, until potatoes are soft. Drain, reserving water. Remove ginger and sprinkle potatoes with allspice. Let cool.

SERVE For babies younger than 9 months, puree in a mini food processor, using reserved cooking liquid as necessary to achieve desired consistency. For babies over 9 months old, mash with a fork until chunky. For toddlers over 12 months old, leave as is for them to eat as a finger food, sprinkled with another pinch of allspice (optional). Serve warm.

A WORLD OF FLAVOR:
Sweet Potato

Sweet potatoes are a wonderful food for babies. The starchy tuber with bright orange flesh is high in vitamin A and beta carotene, and its sweet flavor appeals to tiny taste buds and pairs well with many herbs and spices, especially oregano, cumin powder, and any curry powder blend. When you are short on time, spice up jarred sweet potato baby food by stirring in the desired seasoning and serving.

Potatoes with Lemon and Saffron

MOROCCO MAKES ABOUT 1 CUP

1 medium to large russet potato, peeled and cut in half

Pinch Spanish saffron threads

Salt to taste

⅛ teaspoon freshly squeezed lemon juice

½–1 teaspoon olive oil

Situated in northern Africa across the Mediterranean Sea from the Iberian Peninsula, Morocco is a nation of varied climates, topography, and cultural influences. And it's home to a lot of wonderful flavors, from turmeric to cinnamon to preserved lemons. One of the most iconic is saffron, which, combined with freshly squeezed lemon, transforms these mashed potatoes into an exciting, yummy North African dish.

MAKE Place potato in a 2-quart saucepan and cover with water. Boil over high heat, covered, for 20 minutes, or until fork-tender. Drain, reserving cooking water. Process potato through a ricer, or mash with a fork. In a small bowl, combine 2 tablespoons reserved cooking water and saffron. Mash saffron with the back of a spoon until the color emerges. Add to mashed potatoes, along with salt and lemon juice. Combine gently with a spoon. Add more reserved cooking water if necessary to thin potato mixture.

SERVE Drizzle with olive oil. Serve warm.

Roasted Sweet Potatoes with Cinnamon and Lime

CENTRAL AND SOUTH AMERICA MAKES ABOUT 2 CUPS

Babies around the world *love* sweet potatoes. Cinnamon and lime are typical seasonings used in the Caribbean and Central and South America, from Jamaica to Mexico to Brazil.

3 cups peeled, chopped sweet potato (about 2 large potatoes)

1 tablespoon olive oil

½ teaspoon ground cinnamon

1 teaspoon freshly squeezed lime juice

MAKE Preheat oven to 400°F. In a bowl, toss sweet potatoes, olive oil, and cinnamon. Transfer to a baking sheet and roast for 25 to 30 minutes.

SERVE Puree in a mini food processor, adding water as necessary. Stir in lime juice and serve.

Purple Potato Mash

PERU MAKES ABOUT 1 CUP

The vibrant purple color of these potatoes is exciting to children and grown-ups alike. These little tubers originated in South America, where they are regularly served alongside rich stews as a side dish.

4 small purple potatoes, peeled and cut in half

1 tablespoon minced cilantro

Butter to taste

Salt to taste

Squeeze of lime juice, optional

MAKE In a 2-quart saucepan, place potatoes and enough water to cover them. Bring to a boil over medium-high heat and cook for 10 to 15 minutes, until fork-tender. Drain. Pass potatoes through a ricer or mash with a fork until smooth, adding water as necessary.

SERVE Stir in cilantro, butter, and salt. Add lime juice (if using). Serve warm.

PURPLE
POTATO
MASH

Courgette and Potato Mash

FRANCE MAKES ABOUT 2 CUPS

½ leek

1 to 2 teaspoons butter or olive oil

1 zucchini, peeled and sliced into rounds

½ cup peeled and diced potatoes

Pinch salt (optional)

PREP Clean leek thoroughly to remove sand: Fill a bowl with cold water. Peel off outer layers of leek and chop off root base. Slice into rounds, using the white and light green parts and discarding the dark green tops. Place leek slices in water and swirl with your fingers. The sand will fall to the bottom. When clean, scoop out leeks and place on a clean dish towel to dry. Use about ½ cup for this recipe.

MAKE In a 2-quart saucepan, heat butter or oil over medium-low heat. Once butter foams or oil is hot, add leeks, zucchini, and potatoes. Sauté for 7 to 10 minutes, or until soft, adding a few teaspoons of water as necessary to prevent sticking.

SERVE Mash vegetables with a potato masher or puree in a mini food processor, adding water as necessary to achieve a smooth consistency. Season with salt, if desired, and serve warm or at room temperature.

On a recent trip to France, I scoured baby food aisles and restaurant menus to find out what French babies like to eat. One dish appeared repeatedly—a courgette (pronounced "core-*zhet*") puree, which is a classic French dish. Because courgettes are quite watery when steamed or boiled, I mix them with mashed potatoes and butter for a thicker consistency. Leeks, another aromatic French favorite, give the dish a mild onion taste. Garlic can also be added as your baby's palate develops.

Papas Chorreadas

COLOMBIA MAKES ABOUT 2 CUPS

Papas chorreadas (pronounced "*pa*-pus chore-ray-*ah*-das") is a Colombian potato dish in which small red potatoes are smothered with a rich cheese sauce. Once your baby is ready, add a pinch of ground cumin or chopped cilantro.

1 red potato

¼ cup finely diced onion

1 teaspoon olive oil

½ cup finely chopped tomatoes

1 tablespoon sour cream

1 cup shredded cheddar cheese

Pinch ground black pepper

MAKE In a 1-quart saucepan of water, boil potato over medium-high heat for about 15 minutes. Drain, reserving water. Let cool, peel, and cut into bite-size chunks. In a sauté pan over medium heat, sauté onion in oil until translucent. Add tomatoes. Cook for 5 minutes. Add sour cream. Turn off heat. Stir in cheese, pepper, and potatoes.

SERVE Puree in a mini food processor with a little water. Serve warm.

Isu

NIGERIA MAKES ABOUT 1 CUP

The simplicity of *isu* (pronounced "ee-*shoe*") is wonderful. The dish is gently spiced, which is easy on babies. Cinnamon and garlic are boiled with yams, infusing the cooking water with flavor. Don't forget to wash the yams before you peel them.

2 yams, peeled

½ cinnamon stick

½ garlic clove

Unsalted butter to taste

MAKE In a 2-quart saucepan of water, boil yams, cinnamon, and garlic over medium-high heat for 20 to 25 minutes. Drain. Discard cinnamon and garlic.

SERVE Pass potatoes through a ricer. Drizzle with butter. Serve.

Creamed Corn with Cilantro

CENTRAL AMERICA MAKES ABOUT 10 OUNCES

2 ears fresh corn

1 tablespoon unsalted butter or olive oil

¼ cup diced onion

1 teaspoon minced garlic

¾ cup whole milk, chicken broth, or water

1 teaspoon chopped cilantro

Try this simple but flavorful dish with a pinch of ground coriander, a pinch of ground cumin, or a pinch of curry powder if you want an extra kick. A pinch of chili powder adds dimension without making it too spicy for your little one.

PREP Use a sharp knife to cut corn kernels off cobs. You should have about 2 cups.

MAKE In a 2-quart saucepan, heat butter over medium-low heat for 2 to 3 minutes. Add onions and cook, stirring, for about 3 minutes, or until translucent. Stir in garlic and sauté for 30 seconds. Add corn and milk. Bring to a boil, reduce heat to low, and simmer gently for 10 minutes, or until mixture thickens a bit and corn is cooked.

SERVE Add cilantro. For babies younger than 9 months, puree in a mini food processor to make an appropriate consistency. Leave as is for babies over 9 months old. Serve warm.

A WORLD OF FLAVOR:
Corn

Corn is one of the most important ingredients in Central and South American cooking. It is used in everything from soups to tortillas to sweet and savory puddings. Its natural milk and starches help create a creamy consistency that's just right for babies.

Sweet Corn, Bean, and Coconut Milk Stew

BELIZE MAKES ABOUT 3 CUPS

Belizean cuisine is a big melting pot of flavors, with influences from Spanish, Creole, Chinese, and even British cuisine. Beans, rice, and coconut milk are staple ingredients that are all eaten in some form for breakfast, lunch, and dinner. Here is a recipe that incorporates all three.

⅓ cup dried kidney beans

1 teaspoon olive oil

½ cup diced onion

1 garlic clove, mashed

1–2 thin slices fresh ginger

½ cup fresh or frozen sweet corn

¼ cup diced green bell pepper

Pinch ground cumin

Pinch oregano (preferably Mexican)

2 tablespoons coconut milk

PREP Soak beans overnight in a generous amount of water. The next morning, drain them.

MAKE Place beans and 4 cups water in a 2-quart saucepan. Boil for 45 to 55 minutes, until soft. Beans should be covered by an inch of water; if too much evaporates, add more. Toward the end of cooking time, mash beans with a wooden spoon or potato masher.

In another 2-quart saucepan, heat oil over medium-low heat. Add onions and sauté for 5 to 7 minutes, until soft. Add remaining ingredients. Cover and simmer on low heat until flavors have incorporated and peppers have softened, about 10 minutes.

SERVE For babies younger than 9 months, puree in a blender with a little water as necessary. Mash mixture with the back of a spoon for babies over 9 months old. Serve warm or at room temperature.

Locro

PERU MAKES ABOUT 3 CUPS

1 small sugar pumpkin or other squash (acorn and butternut work well)

1 teaspoon olive oil

½ cup diced onion

1 teaspoon minced garlic

1 tablespoon tomato paste

1 cup peeled and diced russet potatoes

½ cup sweet corn, fresh or frozen

Pinch ground nutmeg

Pinch dried oregano

Pinch salt, optional

Locro (pronounced *"low*-croh") is a thick stew enjoyed in Ecuador, Peru, and Argentina. It is prepared differently in each country—in Ecuador, it is made with potato and cheese stew, while in Argentina, hominy, meat, and potato are used. Pumpkin is a popular choice to use in Peru's squash-based version, and it's used here for a hint of sweetness, which babies love. For thicker stew, add 2 to 3 tablespoons whole milk or unsweetened evaporated milk toward the end of cooking time.

PREP Peel and seed pumpkin and chop into bite-sized chunks. In a 2-quart saucepan, place pumpkin and cover with water. Bring to a boil over high heat, reduce heat to medium-low, and cook, covered, for 10 to 15 minutes, or until soft. Set aside to cool.

MAKE In another 2-quart saucepan, heat oil over medium heat and sauté onion for 5 to 7 minutes, until soft. Add garlic and cook for 1 minute. Add tomato paste and cook for an additional 1 to 2 minutes. Add potatoes, corn, and enough water to cover everything. Boil for 10 to 15 minutes, until potatoes are soft. Add cooked pumpkin, nutmeg, oregano, and salt (if using) and simmer for an additional 5 minutes to allow flavors to come together.

SERVE For babies younger than 9 months, puree in a mini food processor with a little water. Mash with potato masher for babies over 9 months old.

Petit Pois à la Française

FRANCE MAKES ABOUT 1½ CUPS

¼ teaspoon butter

1 teaspoon olive oil

½ cup peeled and sliced yellow onion (slice in rings)

½–1 cup frozen petite peas

1–2 leaves Boston or red leaf lettuce

Pinch salt

Pinch ground black pepper

MAKE In a frying pan, heat butter and oil over medium-low heat. Add onions and sauté for about 10 to 15 minutes, until they caramelize, turning a dark brown color. Stir occasionally and add a few drops of water as necessary to prevent sticking. Add peas, lettuce, salt, and pepper. Cook for about 3 to 5 minutes, until peas are tender and lettuce is wilted. Let cool.

SERVE Transfer mixture to a blender and puree, adding a bit of water as necessary to achieve a smooth consistency. Serve warm or at room temperature.

Peas are their best in the French style—sautéed with onions, lettuce, and a little butter and sprinkled with salt and pepper. Although onions might sound like a strong flavor to feed a little one, in this recipe they are caramelized, which brings out their natural sweetness, making them plenty baby friendly. You can make the onions or the peas the star of the dish, your choice—just adjust the ratio of peas to onions to your baby's liking. (Hint for adults: bacon and cream are delicious additions to this recipe.)

English Peas with a Hint of Mint

UNITED KINGDOM MAKES ABOUT 1 CUP

English peas, also known as garden peas, appear for a short time, usually late spring and early summer. They are sweet and tender, making them a baby favorite. Mint makes them even more flavorful.

1 green onion, trimmed and chopped

1 teaspoon olive oil

1 cup fresh English peas or frozen petite peas

3 fresh mint leaves, washed and minced, or pinch dried mint

MAKE In a 1-quart saucepan over medium-low heat, sauté onions and oil for 3 to 5 minutes. Add peas, mint, and 3 tablespoons water. Cover and steam for about 3 minutes. Let cool.

SERVE Puree in a mini food processor until smooth and serve.

Sukuma Wiki

KENYA MAKES ABOUT 1 CUP

Sukuma wiki (pronounced "skoo-ma wee-key") means "stretch the week" in Swahili, referring to using your resources efficiently to last several days. You can substitute regular kale, collards, or a combination for the baby kale.

1 teaspoon olive oil

1 small onion, chopped (about ¾ cup)

1 cup chopped tomatoes

1 teaspoon all-purpose flour

½ pound baby kale, washed

Salt to taste

MAKE In a sauté pan, heat oil over medium heat. Add onions and sauté for 3 to 5 minutes. Add tomatoes and sauté for 3 minutes. Add flour and stir for 1 minute. Add ½ cup water and kale. Cover and cook for 15 minutes.

SERVE Add salt. Puree in a mini food processor. Serve warm.

Fasoulia

ARMENIA MAKES ABOUT 2 CUPS

1 teaspoon olive oil

½ cup chopped onions

2 garlic cloves, smashed

1 vine-ripened tomato, chopped (about 1½ cups)

1 12-ounce bag washed and trimmed fresh green beans

This mildly flavored stew takes its name from the Arabic word for "beans," the dish's main ingredient. It is popular in several Arabic-speaking countries; some preparations of *fasoulia* (pronounced "fah-*sue*-lee-ah") call for kidney beans, others for ground meat. This green bean version is from Armenia.

MAKE   In a Dutch oven or heavy-bottom pot, heat oil over medium-high heat. Add onions and sauté for 3 minutes. Add garlic and tomatoes and cook for 2 minutes. Add green beans and ½ cup water. Stir and cover. Turn heat to low to maintain a simmer and cook for about 45 minutes, until beans are soft and a thin sauce has formed.

SERVE   For babies 6 to 9 months old, puree in a mini food processor. Serve as is to toddlers.

Poaching guarantees a moist dish flavored with whatever herbs and aromatics are in the cooking liquid. In this recipe, the lemongrass, basil, and even the coconut milk imbue the chicken with quintessential Thai flavors.

A WORLD OF FLAVOR:
Turmeric

Ayurveda is an ancient Indian healing system based on the principle that health and wellness are achieved when the mind, body, and spirit are balanced. Certain foods are said to help with this balance—including turmeric. In the kitchen, it is used to give a pleasantly tart flavor and warm yellow color to curries, rice, vegetables, and meat dishes all over western and southeast Asia. It also is a common spice given to babies in India.

Chicken Poached in Spiced Coconut Milk

THAILAND MAKES 2-3 SERVINGS

½ teaspoon chopped lemongrass

½ teaspoon minced garlic

½ teaspoon minced ginger

3 fresh basil leaves (preferably Thai basil)

1 teaspoon curry powder

½–¾ cup no-sodium chicken stock

1 tablespoon coconut milk

⅛ teaspoon turmeric

2 boneless chicken thighs

PREP   Using a mortar and pestle, grind lemongrass, garlic, ginger, basil, and curry powder into a fragrant paste.

MAKE   In a 2-quart saucepan, stir together stock, coconut milk, turmeric, and most or all of the paste, or less to taste. Add chicken pieces. Chicken should be mostly—but not completely—submerged. Bring to a boil, cover, reduce heat to low, and simmer for 15 to 20 minutes, or until chicken is cooked through.

SERVE   For babies, puree in a mini food processor with a bit of cooking liquid as necessary to achieve desired consistency. Serve minced to toddlers.

Melanzana

ITALY MAKES ABOUT 1 CUP

Melanzana (pronounced "meh-lahn-*zah*-nah") is a flavorful and fast eggplant recipe. It's easy to make, it uses only one pot, and it purees well. Serve as is, as a spread between buttered bread for a tasty sandwich, or as a dip for crackers at snack time. Increase the amounts of spices as your baby gets used to the flavors.

1 teaspoon olive oil

2 eggplants, tops trimmed, diced (about 6 cups)

1½ cups chopped tomatoes

1 teaspoon minced garlic

3 fresh basil leaves or pinch dried basil

MAKE In a skillet, heat oil over medium heat. Add eggplant, tomatoes, and garlic. Cover and cook for 25 minutes, until vegetables are soft.

SERVE Stir in basil. For babies younger than 9 months, puree in a mini food processor. Serve as is for babies over 9 months old.

Épinards et Saumon

FRANCE MAKES ABOUT 1 CUP

1 salmon fillet (about 4 ounces), skin removed

2 cups fresh baby spinach

Pinch dried thyme

Pinch garlic powder

Épinards et saumon (pronounced "eh-*pin*-ard ay soh-*moh*"), or spinach with salmon, is a baby food I've found again and again in French grocery stores. The mixture is well seasoned, and it's easy to make.

MAKE Place salmon on a plate and microwave on high power for 1 to 2 minutes, until fish flakes easily. Place spinach and 3 tablespoons water in a small saucepan. Cook uncovered over medium-low heat, stirring frequently, for about 5 minutes, until just wilted.

SERVE In a mini food processor, puree salmon, spinach, thyme, and garlic powder. Serve warm.

Fish stews, soups, and pies regularly appear on family tables in Finland, Norway, and Sweden. This is a gentle and easy way to introduce your little one to fish.

Milk-Poached Salmon with Dill and Mustard

SCANDINAVIA MAKES ABOUT 1 CUP

1 cup whole milk

¼ teaspoon Dijon mustard

⅛ teaspoon chopped fresh dill

1 salmon fillet (about 4 ounces), skin removed and inspected for bones

MAKE In a small saucepan, stir together milk, mustard, and dill. Heat over medium heat until steaming. Lower heat and place salmon fillet into milk. The milk should reach halfway up the sides of the fish; if necessary, add more milk. Cover and simmer over low heat for 7 to 10 minutes, until fish is cooked through.

SERVE In a mini food processor, puree fish with some of the cooking liquid.

Poached Salmon and Herbs

Try perfuming the poaching milk with any one of these other flavors.

French:
HERBES DE PROVENCE

Spanish:
GARLIC, SAFFRON, SMOKED PAPRIKA

Indian:
CURRY POWDER

Italian:
BASIL, GARLIC, PARSLEY, TOMATO

Chinese:
FIVE-SPICE POWDER, GINGER, STAR ANISE

Moong Dal

INDIA MAKES ABOUT 3 CUPS

½ cup dried split yellow lentils (moong dal)

Pinch turmeric

Pinch salt

This quick-cooking *moong dal* (pronounced "moo-*ng* dahl") is full of protein and can be seasoned any way you wish. After introducing your baby to the basic recipe, try tempering it (see variation and page 91 for more on tempering).

PREP   Inspect lentils carefully, picking out sediment and stones. Place lentils in a 2-quart saucepan. Rinse thoroughly 2 or 3 times. Drain and add 2 cups fresh water.

MAKE   Over medium-high heat, bring lentils, turmeric, and salt to a boil. Cook, partially covered, for 25 to 35 minutes, until soft. Check frequently to make sure mixture does not boil over; if foam appears on top, skim off and discard. Add water if mixture appears to be drying out. Dal is ready when you can mash the lentils with the back of a spoon or break them down with a whisk. After mashing, remove from heat.

SERVE   For babies younger than 9 months, puree with a stick blender. Leave as is for babies over 9 months old. Serve warm.

>Variation

Tempered Moong Dal When dal is nearly done, heat 1 teaspoon ghee in a small saucepan over medium-high heat. When hot, add ½ teaspoon black mustard seeds and ½ teaspoon cumin seeds. Be careful, because the seeds will sputter. Quickly add ¼ cup chopped tomatoes, 1 teaspoon minced garlic, and 1 teaspoon minced ginger. Stir vigorously until tomato starts to soften, break down, and become saucy. Add entire mixture to dal and simmer until flavors come together. Season with salt to taste.

Toovar Dal

INDIA MAKES ABOUT 2 CUPS

Toovar dal (pronounced "*too*-ver dahl") was a childhood favorite of mine. It's a classic dish from Gujarat, a state in western India. If you use the optional jaggery in this recipe, don't skip the lemon, which balances the jaggery's sweetness.

A WORLD OF FLAVOR:
Jaggery

Jaggery is an unrefined sugar made from raw sugarcane juice, date palm, or coconut sap. The juice or sap is boiled down and cooled into block form, which is how it is sold in Asian markets. A baby favorite in India, it contains nutrients and minerals not found in granulated sugar and is even used in Ayurvedic medicine to aid digestion and provide energy.

½ cup dried split yellow pigeon peas (toovar dal)

2 thin slices fresh ginger

Pinch ground turmeric

¼ cup chopped tomatoes

Pinch ground coriander

Pinch ground cumin

⅛ teaspoon jaggery, optional

1 squeeze fresh lemon juice or ½ teaspoon tamarind concentrate

Pinch salt

Ghee for serving, optional

PREP Inspect pigeon peas carefully, picking out sediment and stones. Place peas in a 2-quart saucepan. Rinse thoroughly 2 or 3 times. Drain and add 3 cups fresh water. Soak for a minimum of 4 hours or overnight.

MAKE Drain peas and place in a pot with 4 cups fresh water. Add ginger, turmeric, and tomatoes and bring to a boil over medium-high heat. Cook, partially covered, for 35 to 45 minutes, until peas are soft; watch closely and add more water if peas appear to be drying out. When cooked, mash them with the back of a spoon or break them down with a whisk. Add coriander, cumin, jaggery, lemon juice, and salt. Cook for an additional 1 to 2 minutes. Remove from heat.

SERVE For babies younger than 9 months, puree with a stick blender. Leave as is for babies over 9 months old. Serve warm or at room temperature, topped with a dollop of ghee if desired.

Tempered Toovar Dal

Called *chaunk* in Hindi, tempering is a cooking technique in which whole spices are cooked in a small amount of heated ghee or oil before being poured into a dish. This mixture serves as a garnish of sorts and adds incredible flavor and aroma.

To temper toovar dal: When dal is nearly done, heat 1 teaspoon ghee in a small frying pan over medium-high heat. Add a pinch of whole black mustard seeds, a pinch of whole cumin seeds, and 1 whole clove. When spices sputter, immediately transfer mixture to dal. Be careful because dal will sputter when it comes in contact with the hot ghee. Cook dal with spices for an additional 1 to 2 minutes and serve.

Get creative with your tempering—try slices of garlic, ginger, cloves, and/or asafetida, an essential Indian spice.

Lime-Scented Coconut Rice

THAILAND MAKES ABOUT 1 CUP

½ cup jasmine rice

½ cup coconut milk

1–2 fresh makrut lime leaves or 1 teaspoon freshly squeezed lime juice

PREP Place rice in a 2-quart saucepan and cover with plenty of water. Using clean hands, swirl rice in pot and scrub with fingers. When water turns cloudy, drain rice and add fresh water. Repeat several times until water is mostly clear. Drain.

MAKE Add ½ cup fresh water and coconut milk to the pot. Bring mixture to a boil. Reduce heat to low, cover, and simmer for about 10 minutes. Place makrut leaves on top of rice or add lime juice. Cover and finish cooking for an additional 5 minutes, until rice is soft. Remove and discard leaves.

SERVE For younger babies, puree in a mini food processor with a little coconut milk or water. Leave as is for babies over 9 months old. Serve warm or at room temperature.

Rice is a common first food throughout Southeast Asia. Although babies might start with plain rice porridge or rice water for their very first bites, the flavors that the rest of their families are enjoying are quickly added. Makrut leaves and coconut make this dish distinctly Thai. Makrut leaves come from an Indonesian/Thai lime tree and are used to perfume curries, marinades, and rice. When combined with coconut milk, the rice develops a mellow, but bright, sweet, and slightly sour flavor. For a change from makrut leaves, flavor the rice with fresh curry leaves or Thai basil.

Curried Coconut Rice

SOUTHEAST ASIA MAKES ABOUT 2 CUPS

Curry means different things in different countries. In Thailand, it's usually meat and/or vegetables stewed in coconut milk with a spice paste. In India and Pakistan, it may be dry, consisting of meat or vegetables lightly coated with a seasoned paste, or wet, served with a gravy thinned with yogurt or coconut milk. This recipe, which blends coconut milk and spices, is typical of Thai, Malaysian, and south Indian curries.

A WORLD OF FLAVOR:
Curry Powder

The spice mix sold as curry powder in the west is usually a blend of turmeric, coriander, pepper, cumin, and cloves. Curry powder in India or Southeast Asia, however, is a whole other beast. Any given blend can include up to twenty or thirty spices!

1 teaspoon olive oil

½ cup basmati or jasmine rice

Pinch Spanish saffron threads or ⅛ teaspoon turmeric

Pinch curry powder

Pinch salt, optional

¾ cup no-sodium organic chicken broth or water

½ cup coconut milk

MAKE Place oil, rice, saffron, curry powder, and salt (if using) in a 2-quart saucepan and stir to coat grains. Toast over medium heat until grains turn slightly brown. Lower heat and slowly add broth and coconut milk. Be careful because mixture will sputter. Stir 2 to 3 times, lower heat, cover, and simmer for 7 to 10 minutes. Check occasionally to ensure rice is not sticking to pan. Then remove from heat and let rice rest for 5 minutes.

SERVE For babies younger than 9 months, puree in a mini food processor with a little bit of water or coconut milk as necessary. Serve as is for babies over 9 months old.

Blue Islands Coconut Rice

CARIBBEAN MAKES ABOUT 1 CUP

½ cup basmati rice
½ cup coconut milk
Pinch freshly grated nutmeg

PREP Place rice in a 2-quart saucepan and cover with plenty of water. Using clean hands, swirl rice in pot and scrub with fingers. When water turns cloudy, drain rice and add fresh water. Repeat several times until water is mostly clear. Drain.

MAKE Add ¾ cup fresh water and coconut milk to the pot with rice. Bring to a boil, then cover and reduce heat to a simmer. Cook for 15 minutes, or until rice grains are soft.

SERVE Once rice is cooked, stir in grated nutmeg. Serve warm or at room temperature.

It's hard to pinpoint just one island nation that uses this recipe. One thing is for sure: Caribbean babies are introduced to seasoned rice at an early age—and it's never from a box! Nutmeg is a staple spice in Caribbean cooking, and basmati rice is a typical fragrant grain. Together with coconut milk, a common cooking liquid in the region, they're a burst of tropical flavors for your baby. For softer or "wetter" rice, simply add a few tablespoons of water or coconut milk to the cooked rice and mix vigorously to break up the grains, creating a more porridgelike consistency.

In Japan, when a baby turns 100 days old the milestone is celebrated with a ceremony called *Okuizome*, which means "first meal," to bless the baby with an abundant life. Often the ceremonial meal includes *sekihan* (pronounced "*secky*-haan"), a rice dish often served at birthdays, holidays, and other special occasions. It's a Japanese version of red beans and rice featuring adzuki beans, which have a beautiful, deep red color and are commonly used in desserts.

Sekihan

JAPAN MAKES ABOUT 2 CUPS

½ cup dried adzuki beans

2 cups Japanese sweet rice

PREP Pick over beans for small stones or detritus and then rinse. Place in a bowl with 3–4 cups water and set aside to soak overnight.

In another bowl, place rice and rinse with cold water, swirling rice with clean fingers to remove any dust or impurities. Drain rice and add fresh water. Repeat several times, until water runs clear. After the final rinse, add 3–4 cups water and soak rice overnight as well.

The next morning, drain liquid from both bowls.

MAKE In a 2-quart saucepan, place beans and 2 cups fresh water. Cover and bring to a boil over medium-high heat. Cook for about 30 to 45 minutes, until soft. Drain beans, reserving cooking water. Transfer beans to another 2-quart saucepan and add drained rice. Add 3 cups cooking liquid, using reserved bean water and as much additional water as necessary. Bring to a boil over high heat, then cover and reduce heat to medium-low. Cook for 25 minutes. Lower heat to maintain a simmer and cook for an additional 20 to 25 minutes, or until rice is soft.

SERVE For babies younger than 9 months, puree in a mini food processor with a little water as necessary or mash with a potato masher. Leave as is for older babies. Serve warm.

Uncle Sanjay's Curried Baked Beans

UNITED KINGDOM MAKES ABOUT ½ CUP

1 teaspoon olive oil

2 tablespoons minced onions

2 teaspoons minced garlic

1 4-ounce can baked beans

½ teaspoon garam masala

Curry is a big deal in the U.K.: chicken tikka masala has been the national dish of England since 2001. Inspired by dear friends in London, I've doctored these baked beans with onions, garlic, curry powder, and some chilies. The curry spices go a long way to mellow the sweetness of the baked beans.

MAKE In a sauté pan, heat oil over medium heat. Add onions and sauté for 3 to 5 minutes, until translucent and fragrant. Add garlic and stir for 30 seconds. Add beans, garam masala, and a splash of water, then lower heat and cover. Simmer for 5 minutes.

SERVE For younger babies, puree in a mini food processor. Serve as is to toddlers.

Habichuelas con dulce (pronounced "ah-bee-*chweh*-lahs cawn *dool-seh*") traditionally is served in many Dominican households during Lent and also as a food for babies. This baby-friendly version uses a bit less milk and sugar than the original; the sweet potatoes and raisins lend natural sweetness. And it's packed with nutrition—protein and fiber from the beans and vitamin A and beta-carotene from the sweet potato.

Habichuelas con Dulce

DOMINICAN REPUBLIC MAKES ABOUT 3 CUPS

1 cup dried kidney beans

2 tablespoons unsulphured raisins

½ cup peeled and diced sweet potatoes

1 cup coconut milk

Pinch ground cinnamon

Pinch ground cloves

PREP Pick over kidney beans for small stones and detritus and then rinse. Place in a bowl with a generous amount of water and soak overnight. The next morning, drain beans and discard liquid.

MAKE In a 2-quart saucepan, place beans, 4 cups water, and raisins. Bring to a boil over medium-high heat and cook, adding water if the level over the beans drops to less than an inch, for 45 to 55 minutes, until soft. Toward the end of cooking time, mash beans with a wooden spoon or potato masher.

In a 1-quart saucepan over medium-high heat, bring sweet potatoes and enough water to cover them to a boil. Cover, reduce heat to medium-low, and steam for about 7 to 10 minutes, until potatoes are soft. Drain and set aside. Transfer cooked beans and potatoes to a mini food processor and puree with a little water to achieve a thick, souplike consistency. Use a strainer to remove pieces of skins and other solids. Return strained mixture to pot and add coconut milk, cinnamon, and cloves. Cook for 10 to 15 minutes over medium heat, until mixture reduces a bit and is creamy.

SERVE Serve warm or at room temperature.

Shorbat Adas

IRAQ/LEBANON MAKES ABOUT 2 CUPS

Shorbat adas (pronounced "shore-*bhutt ah*-das"), which means "lentil soup" in Arabic, is one of the easiest, tastiest lentil preparations I have encountered. This recipe uses split red lentils (masoor dal), which are common to India and all over the Middle East, where they are cooked with similar seasonings in each region. This baby-friendly version is great with a bowl of rice. As your baby's taste buds mature, start adding more spices—like a pinch each of ground cumin and ground coriander in the last few minutes of cooking time.

½ cup dried split red lentils (masoor dal)

2 thin slices fresh ginger

⅛ teaspoon minced garlic

Pinch salt

Pinch turmeric

½ teaspoon ghee for serving

PREP Inspect lentils carefully, picking out sediment and stones. Place lentils in a 2-quart saucepan. Rinse thoroughly 2 or 3 times. Drain lentils, discarding liquid.

MAKE In a large pot, bring lentils, 2 cups fresh water, ginger, garlic, salt, and turmeric to a boil over medium-high heat. Cook, partially covered, for 15 to 20 minutes, until soft enough to be mashed. Add more water if lentils appear to be drying out. Mash lentils with the back of a spoon or break down with a whisk. Let cool for 5 minutes.

SERVE Puree mixture with a stick blender, adding water if necessary to create a thick souplike consistency. Serve as is or add spoonfuls to fruit or vegetable purees. Add a dollop of ghee for extra flavor.

Puré de Verduras

SPAIN MAKES ABOUT 2 CUPS

3 small russet potatoes

1 zucchini

1 carrot

Pinch Spanish saffron threads

Pinch sweet paprika (or smoked paprika)

Pinch salt, optional

PREP Peel and chop potatoes, zucchini, and carrots.

MAKE In a 2-quart saucepan, place vegetables and enough water to cover them by about an inch. Bring to a boil over medium-high heat and cook for 15 to 20 minutes, until soft. Drain, reserving water.

SERVE In a mini food processor, puree vegetables with saffron and paprika, adding reserved water as necessary to achieve a smooth consistency. Stir in salt, if desired, and serve.

Puré de verduras (pronounced "*pu*-ray day ver-*du*-ras") is a popular Spanish soup served as a starter before dinner. Soft, smooth, and flavorful, it is packed with nutrients and makes a wonderful first food for babies. Don't forget to wash the vegetables before peeling them. Saffron and paprika provide gentle flavor and color the dish. You can add other seasonings as your baby accepts them.

Nohut Çorbasi

TURKEY MAKES ABOUT 2 CUPS

From seasoned kebabs to weakened black tea, Turkish children regularly eat what their parents are eating. That includes soup, a large part of Turkish cuisine. This chickpea soup, *nohut çorbasi* (pronounced "no-*hoot* chore-*bus-suh*"), is soft, smooth, and highly nutritious, a wonderful baby food.

1 cup dried chickpeas

1 teaspoon unsalted butter

1 teaspoon olive oil

½ cup chopped red bell pepper

1 carrot, peeled and chopped

½ cup diced onions

⅛ teaspoon ground cinnamon

⅛ teaspoon ground paprika

⅛ teaspoon ground cumin

1 sprig fresh coriander leaves

PREP Soak chickpeas in 3 cups water overnight. Drain.

MAKE In a large pot over medium-high heat, bring chickpeas and plenty of water to a boil. Cook, covered, for 50 minutes, until soft. Drain, reserving water. In a frying pan, heat butter and oil over medium heat. Add peppers, carrots, and onions and sauté for 10 to 15 minutes, until soft. Add chickpeas and seasonings and cook for 5 to 7 minutes. Add about 1 cup reserved cooking water.

SERVE Blend with a stick blender until smooth. Serve warm.

Baby Ratatouille Provençal

FRANCE MAKES ABOUT 3 CUPS

1 teaspoon olive oil

½ cup diced onion

1 teaspoon minced garlic

⅓ cup chopped Roma tomatoes

⅓ cup diced zucchini

⅓ cup diced eggplant

⅓ cup diced green peppers

⅓ cup fresh or frozen diced carrots

Pinch herbes de Provence or any combination of rosemary,
    sage, marjoram, and/or thyme

Pinch salt, optional

Provençal alludes to the style of cooking in southern France, which features dishes lovingly prepared with fresh olive oil, garlic, and olives. A ratatouille (pronounced "rah-ta-*too*-wee") is a tasty mélange of vegetables cooked in garlic-infused olive oil and typically served with warm, crusty bread. With some minor adjustments—mainly reducing the amount of fat—ratatouille is a wonderful baby food.

MAKE In a sauté pan, heat oil on medium-low heat. When hot, add onion and cook for about 5 minutes, until onion becomes translucent. Add garlic and sauté for 30 seconds. Add tomatoes and cook for 2 minutes, or until tomatoes break down. Add remaining vegetables and stir to coat all the vegetables in oil. Add ⅓ cup water, cover, and simmer until everything is soft, 10 to 15 minutes. Add spices and salt (if using) and cook for an additional 1 to 2 minutes.

SERVE For young babies, let mixture cool and then puree. Serve as is for babies 9 months and older.

Baby Minestrone Soup

ITALY MAKES ABOUT 2 CUPS

Soups are popular the world over as a baby's first food, whether brothy and light or pureed and smooth. You can serve minestrone soup to your baby in either form. It's an excellent way to introduce seasonal vegetables and Italian flavors and use up leftover cooked pasta and beans.

1 teaspoon olive oil

⅓ cup diced onion

1 teaspoon minced garlic

½ cup diced tomatoes

⅓ cup canned cannellini or kidney beans, rinsed and drained

⅓ cup frozen chopped spinach

⅓ cup frozen diced carrots or mixed vegetables

1 cup no-sodium chicken or vegetable stock

⅛ teaspoon dried oregano

⅛ teaspoon dried basil

2 tablespoons cooked whole-wheat pasta (such as small shells or ditalini)

MAKE In a 2-quart saucepan, heat oil over medium heat. Add onions and sauté for 5 to 7 minutes, until translucent and soft. Add garlic and tomatoes and cook for about 3 minutes, or until tomatoes break down. Add beans, spinach, carrots, stock, oregano, and basil. Simmer for 5 to 7 minutes to allow flavors to come together. Add pasta and simmer for an additional 1 to 2 minutes. Let cool.

SERVE For babies younger than 9 months, puree in a blender. Leave as is for babies over 9 months old. Serve warm or at room temperature.

PUMPKIN
FENNEL
ÇORBASI

Avocado Soup with Lime and Cilantro

CENTRAL AND SOUTH AMERICA MAKES ABOUT 1 CUP

2 avocados, pit removed, fleshed scooped out

1 tablespoon lime juice

1 tablespoon chopped cilantro

Pinch ground cumin

Usually served chilled, Central and South American avocado soup can be seasoned with chili, lime, cumin, and/or cilantro. This baby-friendly version features fresh cilantro and lime and comes together in less than 10 minutes.

MAKE In a mini food processor, place avocado flesh, lime juice, cilantro, and cumin. Puree, adding water until thick and souplike.

SERVE Serve chilled.

Pumpkin Fennel Çorbasi

TURKEY MAKES ABOUT 2 CUPS

Pinch cumin seeds

Pinch cardamom seeds

Pinch fennel seeds

1 tablespoon olive oil

⅓ cup diced onion

1 8-ounce can pumpkin puree

Pinch salt, optional

Cinnamon and allspice may be classic seasonings for pumpkin, but other spices pair well with this popular squash. The fennel seeds in this smooth and savory soup add their signature anise flavor and aroma.

MAKE With a mortar and pestle, grind all spices into a powder. In a 2-quart saucepan, heat oil over medium-low heat. Add onions and sauté for 5 to 7 minutes, until they start to brown. Add spices and pumpkin. Stir for 2 minutes. Add ⅓ cup water and salt (if using). Simmer for 10 to 15 minutes.

SERVE Puree in a blender. Serve warm or at room temperature.

Hungarian Apple Soup

HUNGARY MAKES ABOUT 1 CUP

Popular in Eastern Europe, fruit soups are wonderful for new taste buds. The sweetness and familiarity of a fruit like apple provide a pleasing backdrop for introducing flavors such as paprika, a cornerstone of Hungarian cooking. Onion and sage, typical of Hungarian cuisine, are bold flavors, so add them in small amounts to start if your baby isn't accustomed to them. And be sure to wash the apple and potato before peeling them.

A WORLD OF FLAVOR:
Paprika

Hungarian paprika, a deep red powder made of ground red pepper pods, comes in many intensities. Sweet paprika is the most baby friendly, bringing a rich pepper flavor and crimson color without any heat.

2 red apples, any variety

1 teaspoon olive oil

1 tablespoon diced onion, optional

½ cup peeled and diced russet potato (about 1 small potato)

Pinch Hungarian sweet paprika

Pinch dried sage, optional

1 cup no-sodium chicken broth or water

PREP   Peel and dice apples.

MAKE   In a 2-quart saucepan, heat oil over medium heat. Add onions (if using) and sauté for 2 minutes. Add apples, potatoes, paprika, and sage (if using). Sauté for 3 to 5 minutes, stirring frequently to prevent sticking. Add broth and bring to a boil. Cover, reduce heat to low, and simmer for about 15 minutes, or until apples and vegetables are soft. Let cool for 5 minutes.

SERVE   Puree with a stick blender or mini food processor.

Blueberry Soup

POLAND/FINLAND/SWEDEN MAKES ABOUT 2 CUPS

1 pint fresh or frozen blueberries

¼ teaspoon ground cinnamon

2 teaspoons rice flour (or other starch)

1 teaspoon sugar, optional

Sour or whipped cream, for serving

This soup is a fruity treat for babies and adults alike. It can be served cold or warm and couldn't be simpler to make. In Sweden it's popular with chilly skiers, who tuck it away in a thermos. I thicken the soup with a bit of rice flour, but you can substitute potato starch, cornstarch, or even cooked rice.

MAKE In a 2-quart saucepan, bring blueberries, cinnamon, rice flour, sugar (if using), and 2 cups water to a boil over medium-high heat. Lower heat and simmer for 10 to 15 minutes.

SERVE Puree with a stick blender or transfer to a mini food processor and puree. Serve warm or cold, with a dollop of sour or whipped cream.

A Spoonful of Flavor

For Babies 7–9 Months and Up

Shaved ice is a popular cooling treat in many tropical countries and locales. Scrape off shavings or fill an ice cube tray with the puree and freeze for later.

A WORLD OF FLAVOR:
Pineapple

Pineapple is readily available, fresh or frozen. Avoid canned pineapple, which may be loaded with extra sugar. Fresh, ripe pineapples will smell sweet and fragrant, and they'll be firm to the touch but yield slightly when pressed.

Watermelon Pineapple Ice

CENTRAL AMERICA MAKES ABOUT 1 CUP

1 cup watermelon chunks
½ cup fresh or frozen pineapple chunks
Pinch freshly chopped mint leaves, optional

MAKE   In a mini food processor, puree watermelon, pineapple, and mint (if using). Pour puree into a small freezer-safe bowl and place in freezer. Chill for 10 minutes.

SERVE   When ready to serve, thaw for 2 to 3 minutes. Mixture will resemble a shaved ice or slush. With a spoon, scrape shavings into a bowl and serve.

Although this isn't true ice cream, it is quick kitchen magic: just two ingredients and no egg yolks, ice cream makers, or complicated gadgets required. Babies' gums are soothed, and older kids—and parents—can get their ice cream fix.

Peach Teething "Ice Cream"

EUROPE MAKES ABOUT 1 CUP

1 cup frozen peach slices
Granulated sugar to taste

MAKE   Place peaches in a mini food processor and sprinkle them with a bit of sugar. Blend, pausing occasionally to scrape down the sides with a rubber spatula, until mixture has a consistency similar to sorbet.

SERVE   Serve immediately.

Cinnamon Avocado Banana Cream

MEXICO/CARIBBEAN MAKES ABOUT 8 OUNCES

1 ripe avocado

1 ripe banana, peeled and cut in half

2 tablespoons (1 ounce) water, breast milk, plain whole-milk yogurt, or formula

1–2 tablespoons plain whole milk yogurt, optional

Pinch ground cinnamon

PREP Cut avocado in half with a sharp knife. Press the knife blade into the pit until it's firmly in place, then twist gently. The pit should pop out. Scoop out flesh with a spoon.

MAKE Place avocado, banana, water, and yogurt (if using) in a mini food processor. Puree until creamy.

SERVE Transfer puree to a small bowl and stir in cinnamon. Serve the same day; store in refrigerator if not serving immediately.

This sweet, creamy dish evokes the Caribbean, pairing tropical avocado and banana with cinnamon, a popular seasoning in local cuisine. It should be served the day it's made, but you can make it a few hours in advance; stir in ½ teaspoon fresh lemon juice to keep the bright green avocado from turning brown, and then refrigerate puree until ready to serve.

A WORLD OF FLAVOR:
Avocado

Avocado's mild flavor and creamy texture make it an ideal first food. This fruit is packed with nutrients including potassium, vitamin K, folate, and monounsaturated fats (regarded as the good kind of fat). When ripe, avocados can simply be cut open, mashed, and served. When ripe, the skin will be dark green, almost black, and you should feel a slight give when you squeeze the avocado. If it is too firm, let it ripen on the countertop for a few days.

Rosewater Vanilla Smoothie

IRAN MAKES 8 OUNCES

Babies and toddlers love smoothies. Sadly, commercially made versions are often loaded with extra sugar and feature only simple fruit flavors. Making smoothies at home allows you to control the sugar and experiment with different fruits and seasonings. In this recipe, enticing vanilla and a few drops of aromatic rosewater take your baby on a culinary adventure to Iran.

1-inch piece vanilla bean or pinch vanilla powder
½ cup plain whole-milk yogurt
2 tablespoons whole milk
¾ teaspoon granulated sugar
⅛ teaspoon rosewater
1–2 ice cubes

PREP If using vanilla bean, use a sharp knife to cut in half. With the edge of the knife, scrape inside of pod, collecting the seeds. Reserve pod for another use.

MAKE In a mini food processor, blend yogurt, milk, sugar, and rosewater. Add vanilla seeds and ice, and blend until smooth and frothy.

SERVE Serve immediately.

> *Variation*

Fruity Smoothie Replace vanilla and rosewater with a combination of spices and fruits: a pinch of ground cardamom or cinnamon, 2 to 3 whole strawberries, ½ banana, and/or ½ cup fresh or defrosted frozen mango chunks. Dried dates with rosewater is another tasty combination.

A WORLD OF FLAVOR:
Rose

Throughout much of the world, especially the Middle East, Pakistan, and Turkey, rose is often used in both sweet and savory dishes. Its gentle, aromatic flavor is incomparable. The petals are used to make rose syrups, which can be added to cakes and desserts, and rosewater, which is used to gently flavor milk and other drinks.

Fruit Lassi

INDIA MAKES ABOUT 8 OUNCES

1 cup fresh, ripe, peeled mango chunks, 1 cup defrosted frozen mango chunks, or 1 cup fruit chunks of your choice

½ cup plain whole-milk yogurt

Pinch ground cardamom or ground cinnamon

1–2 dashes rosewater

MAKE In a mini food processor, blend mango, yogurt, and cardamom. The lassi should be slightly thinner than a milkshake; if necessary, thin with a little whole milk or water.

SERVE Stir in rosewater and serve.

>Variation

Cardamom Lassi Omit fruit and increase yogurt to ¾ cup. Stir in a pinch of granulated sugar along with the cardamom. Thin with whole milk if necessary. Add rosewater and serve.

Lassi (pronounced "luh-*see*") is a popular and refreshing drink from India, usually made with yogurt and milk with a little salt, sugar, fruit, or spices. Sweetened with natural fruits and packed with vitamins and proteins, a fruit lassi is ideal for babies. Fresh fruits with high water content—such as ripe papaya, pineapple, or peaches—work best, but frozen fruits work wonderfully, too. In India, mango is the most commonly used fruit. As your baby grows older, you can sprinkle lassi with ground pistachios or ground almonds.

Persimmons with Jujube and Vanilla

CHINA/KOREA/JAPAN MAKES ABOUT 8 OUNCES

2 dried jujubes

2 ripe Fuyu persimmons

Pinch vanilla powder

PREP Rinse jujubes and soak in a bowl of water for 1 hour. Wash persimmons, cut off the tops, and slice evenly.

MAKE In a 1-quart saucepan, place persimmons, jujubes, vanilla powder, and 2 tablespoons water. Simmer over low to medium heat for 5 to 7 minutes. Remove jujubes from pan and discard. Their flavor will have infused the persimmons.

SERVE Puree remaining mixture in a mini food processor and serve.

Jujube (pronounced "*joo-joo*-bee") is one of several names for Korean dates. You might find them labeled as Chinese dates as well. The flavor of this dried fruit is sweet, similar to that of an apple. If you can't find jujubes, substitute about 2 tablespoons of chopped sulfur-/sulfite-free dates, though the flavor won't be the same.

A WORLD OF FLAVOR: Persimmon

Originally from China, persimmons are gorgeous, bright orange fruits that look something like tomatoes. I remember the first time I spotted them in an Asian supermarket. The aroma was so sweet and intriguing I had to pick one up. Two main varieties are Fuyu and Hachiya. Fuyu persimmons are firm and sweet and can be eaten like an apple. Hachiya are more oblong and should be eaten when extremely soft and ripe; otherwise they are quite sour. Both varieties are high in fiber and vitamin C.

Niter Kibbeh

ETHIOPIA MAKES ABOUT 7 TABLESPOONS

Niter kibbeh (pronounced "knee-thur key-bay") is spiced clarified butter that Ethiopian cooks use daily to impart flavor to vegetables, meats, and sauces. It's pure culinary magic. Drizzle it on rice, green beans, lentils, chicken, carrots—whatever you and your baby are eating. It's a tasty and gentle way to introduce new flavors. This version is intended to be baby-friendly, with plenty of seasoning but no heat. Feel free to increase the spices as your baby adjusts to the flavors.

1 stick butter (salted or unsalted)

¼ teaspoon ground cardamom

½-inch stick cinnamon

⅛ teaspoon cumin seeds

⅛ teaspoon fenugreek seeds

⅛ teaspoon ground turmeric

1 clove

¼ cup minced onion

2 thin slices fresh ginger root

MAKE In a 1-quart saucepan, place all ingredients. Cook over low heat for 7 to 10 minutes. During cooking, the butter fat will rise to the top (it will be foamy), and the clarified butter will accumulate in the bottom of the pan. Skim off fat and discard as it accumulates. When foam has subsided, remove from heat and let spices infuse for another 5 to 10 minutes. Strain mixture and pour liquid into a glass jar with a lid.

SERVE Use niter kibbeh as you would use oil or butter: sauté vegetables or meat with it, serve it over rice, mashed potatoes, or mashed lentils, and more. Store niter kibbeh in the refrigerator, where it will solidify, for several weeks.

Mannaya Kasha

RUSSIA/EASTERN EUROPE MAKES ABOUT 6 OUNCES

1 cup whole milk, water, or a combination

Pinch ground cinnamon, ground cardamom, or both

3 tablespoons semolina flour

1 teaspoon seedless jam or fresh berry puree, ideally sugar-free

1 teaspoon unsalted butter, optional

MAKE In a 1-quart saucepan, place milk and cinnamon. Bring to a boil, stirring frequently so milk doesn't stick to the bottom of the pot, and then remove from heat. Whisk in semolina. Return to low heat, stirring and whisking constantly until a porridge starts to form, 3 to 5 minutes.

SERVE Stir in jam and/or optional butter. Serve at once; once cool, porridge can get gummy.

Sweet or Savory Kasha

Replace the cinnamon and/or jam with a combination of other seasonings.

Sweet:

CLOVE   SAFFRON

ALLSPICE   ANISE

NUTMEG

Savory:

PAPRIKA   PARMESAN

GHEE   CURRY POWDER

TOMATO AND BASIL PUREE   CUMIN

Kasha is often thought of as buckwheat porridge, but in parts of Eastern Europe, it's the name of a semolina-based dish often served with berries for breakfast—as in this *mannaya kasha* (pronounced "mun-*nigh*-uh *kah*-shah"). Warm and creamy, this porridge is wonderful for babies. To add flavor, I perfume the milk with cinnamon or cardamom before whisking in the semolina. You can serve the semolina plain, with just the perfumed milk, or with berries for a more authentic kasha.

A WORLD OF FLAVOR:
Semolina

Semolina, the grain used to make pasta, is an ingredient in recipes all over the world. In South India, for example, it's used to make a savory pudding seasoned with ghee and spices. It can also be turned into a sweet pudding called *sheera* when boiled with milk and cardamom.

Vegetable Couscous with Harissa

MOROCCO/TUNISIA MAKES ABOUT 1 CUP

Harissa, a flavorful red chili paste, is considered the national condiment of Tunisia. Although less authentic than the paste, dry harissa spice blends are less spicy and therefore a good alternative for babies.

Butter for coating pan

¼ cup diced onion

¼ cup shredded carrots

1 teaspoon minced garlic

⅛–¼ teaspoon dried harissa spice blend

½ cup dried couscous

1 cup no-sodium chicken or vegetable stock

MAKE Coat the bottom of a 2-quart saucepan with a small amount of butter. Heat over medium-high heat. Add onions, carrots, garlic, and harissa spice blend. Sauté for about 5 minutes. Transfer to a bowl and set aside. Prepare couscous with the stock according to package directions and cook for about 7 minutes, until soft.

SERVE Stir together carrot mixture and couscous. Cover and let rest for 5 minutes. Serve warm or at room temperature.

Fava Beans

EGYPT MAKES ABOUT ¾ CUP

1 cup fava beans, shelled

1 teaspoon olive oil

1 garlic clove, minced

Pinch cumin powder

Also known as broad beans, fresh fava beans are a staple in Egypt and a popular first food for babies. The beans offer good amounts of protein, fiber, iron, and magnesium.

MAKE   In a 2-quart saucepan over high heat, bring 4 cups water to a boil. Add fava beans and boil for 3 minutes. Drain water and place beans in a bowl filled with ice. Let cool. Remove skins and place beans in a mini food processor. In a small sauté pan, heat oil over medium heat. Add garlic and sauté for 1 to 2 minutes. Stir in cumin. Add to beans and puree.

SERVE   Serve warm or at room temperature.

Poached Fish with Saffron

MEDITERRANEAN/ISRAEL MAKES ABOUT 1 CUP

2 cups no-sodium vegetable or chicken stock

1 garlic clove, cut in half

⅛ teaspoon Spanish saffron threads

1 teaspoon lemon juice

1 4-ounce cod fillet

Saffron and lemon are a classic flavor combination in several regions, including the Mediterranean and Israel. Sweet and bright, they perfume the poaching liquid and flavor the cod.

MAKE   In a sauté pan, heat stock, garlic, saffron, and juice over medium heat until steaming. Add fish and more stock, if necessary, so liquid reaches halfway up the fish. Cover, lower heat, and simmer for 5 to 7 minutes, or until fish is opaque and flakes easily. Let cool in poaching liquid.

SERVE   Puree cod in a mini food processor with a bit of liquid. Serve.

Baked Cod with Papaya and Banana

BRAZIL MAKES ABOUT 3 CUPS

As I've learned from mothers around the world, fish is one of the most common foods fed to babies and toddlers. There are Asian fish curries, Spanish fish stews, and countless meals in between. This Brazilian-style fish recipe is sweetened with papaya and banana, and it works well with pineapple, too. It takes almost no time to bake, is easy to puree, and, best of all, is easy to clean up. Double the recipe and add a bit more pepper if you would like to serve this to grown-ups as well.

Butter for cooking fish

2 yellow bananas, ideally not too ripe

2 4-ounce cod fillets

5 thick slices fresh, ripe, peeled papaya

Pinch salt, optional

Pinch ground black pepper

1 lime, cut in half

PREP Preheat oven to 400°F. Line a rimmed baking dish with two layers of foil and rub a thin film of butter all over the foil. Peel bananas and cut in half lengthwise.

MAKE Place cod in the middle of the pan and arrange sliced papaya and bananas closely around fish. Sprinkle fish with salt (if using) and pepper and then add a small pat of butter to the top of each fillet. Squeeze one or both halves of the lime over everything. Bake for 12 to 15 minutes, until fish is opaque and cooked through. Cod should be moist, but a bit firm, and flake easily with a fork. Remove from oven and let cool.

SERVE Puree fruit and fish in a mini food processor. Serve warm.

Lugaw

PHILIPPINES MAKES ABOUT 2 CUPS

1 cup jasmine rice

1 tablespoon vegetable oil

1 cup chopped yellow onions (1 small to medium onion)

2 tablespoons minced garlic

1 tablespoon freshly grated ginger

5½ cups chicken broth, divided

1 cooked chicken breast, shredded

Dash soy sauce

Dash fish sauce

Similar to Chinese congee (page 32), *lugaw* (pronounced "loo-gaw"), also known as *arroz caldo*, is a comforting Filipino porridge beloved by every family member, from the high chair to the head of the table. The rice is stewed with a lightly spiced broth and topped with chicken. Garlic, ginger, soy sauce, and fish sauce provide an indescribable savory element that you and your baby will love.

PREP Place rice in a bowl and wash with plenty of water. Using clean hands, swirl rice and scrub grains with fingers. When water turns cloudy, carefully drain rice and add fresh water, repeating several times until water is mostly clear. Drain and set aside.

MAKE In a 2-quart saucepan, heat oil over medium heat. Add onions and sauté for 2 to 3 minutes. Add garlic and ginger and sauté, stirring frequently to keep garlic from burning, for another 3 to 5 minutes. Add rice and 5 cups broth. Bring to a boil, cover, and lower heat to a simmer. Cook for 25 to 30 minutes, or until soft and porridgelike. Stir occasionally with a wooden spoon to break up grains and prevent mixture from sticking. Add extra broth as necessary if mixture is drying out.

SERVE Stir in chicken, soy sauce, and fish sauce. Serve warm.

>Variation

Lugaw with Eggs As your baby grows, try different toppings and stir-ins like scrambled or chopped hard-boiled eggs, scallions, or even a teeny bit of hot sauce.

Carrot Soba

JAPAN MAKES ABOUT 1 CUP

Buckwheat soba noodles are served all over Japan, both cold, with special dipping sauces, and warm, in tasty soups or broths. They have a slightly nutty flavor and adapt well to a variety of seasonings. Soba's magnesium, fiber, and protein are all good for growing bodies.

½ teaspoon soy sauce

¼ teaspoon sesame oil

Pinch granulated sugar

1 cup soba noodles, cooked according to package directions

½ cup finely shredded carrots

MAKE In a small bowl, mix together soy sauce, sesame oil, and sugar. Rinse and drain cooked soba 2 to 3 times in cold water to wash off excess starch. Return to pan. Turn heat to low. Add carrots and soy sauce mixture. Gently swirl noodles and carrots in pan to incorporate.

SERVE Heat for 1 to 2 minutes, if desired, and serve.

Shiro Wat

ETHIOPIA MAKES ABOUT 1 CUP

Shiro wat (pronounced "*she*-row *what*") is a delicacy in Ethiopian cuisine that's easily adapted for babies. This chickpea flour stew is seasoned with berbere, a spice mixture that typically includes chilies, fenugreek, ginger, and other spices.

¼ onion, finely diced

1 teaspoon olive oil

½ teaspoon minced garlic

Pinch berbere

1 teaspoon tomato paste

½ cup chickpea flour

MAKE In a sauté pan, sauté onion in oil over medium heat for 3 to 5 minutes. Add garlic, berbere, and tomato paste and stir for 1 minute. Add flour and 2 cups water. Cook, stirring constantly, for 10 to 15 minutes, until thick. Add up to 1 additional cup of water if mixture appears dry.

SERVE Serve warm with rice or wheat bread.

Seasoned Lamb Kebabs

TURKEY MAKES ABOUT 10 KEBABS

1 pound ground lamb, preferably grass fed

1 tablespoon vegetable oil

1 small or ½ large onion, finely chopped

1 teaspoon ground coriander

1 teaspoon ground cumin

½ teaspoon salt

¼ cup washed and chopped cilantro

1 teaspoon minced ginger

1 tablespoon minced garlic

1 tablespoon sour cream or whole-milk yogurt

From *doner kebab* in Turkey to skewered garlic-chili kebabs in the Middle East, lamb kebabs are always full of flavor. To appeal to young palates, this family-friendly recipe, inspired by Turkish and Middle Eastern kebabs, omits the fiery green chilies that are commonly used. Add more ginger, garlic, onion, and spices as your baby gets used to these tastes.

PREP Place all ingredients in a bowl and mix with clean hands until well combined. Form mixture into a large ball. Place back in bowl, cover with plastic wrap, and refrigerate for at least 4 hours.

MAKE Preheat oven to 400°F. Line a baking sheet with aluminum foil and take lamb out of the refrigerator. Pull off a tennis-ball-sized amount of meat and form into a log about the size and length of a sausage link or thick hot dog. Place on prepared baking sheet and repeat with the rest of the lamb mixture. Bake for 20 to 25 minutes, or until meat is cooked through and no longer pink in the middle.

SERVE Cut into pieces and serve warm.

>Variation

Grilled Lamb Kebabs Form meat into logs as described above and thread onto skewers. Grill over high heat for about 12 to 15 minutes, rotating every 3 to 4 minutes so all sides cook evenly.

The
Well-Seasoned
High Chair

For Babies 10-12 Months and Up

Lou Rou Fan

TAIWAN MAKES ABOUT 3 CUPS

Lou rou fan (pronounced "lou *row* fahn") is classic Taiwanese comfort food. The star of this minced pork dish is five-spice powder, a popular blend of spices used in Chinese cooking that usually consists of fennel, cinnamon, star anise, cloves, and Szechuan peppercorns. The original dish can be salty, so I've reduced the soy sauce here to make it more baby-friendly. Serve it with rice or noodles.

1 teaspoon vegetable oil

½ cup minced shallots

1 pound ground pork

1 teaspoon minced garlic

1 teaspoon soy sauce

1 teaspoon granulated sugar

½–1 teaspoon five-spice powder

1 teaspoon rice wine vinegar

1 bay leaf

1 ¼ cups no-sodium beef broth or other broth

MAKE   In a sauté pan, heat oil over medium-high heat. Sauté shallots for 2 to 3 minutes. Add pork and garlic and cook for about 5 minutes, until most of the pink is gone from the meat, breaking up pieces with a wooden spoon. Add soy sauce, sugar, five-spice powder, vinegar, bay leaf, and broth. Stir, lower heat, and simmer for 30 minutes to 1 hour.

SERVE   Remove bay leaf. Serve minced pork with noodles, fragrant plain rice, or as is.

Keema

INDIA/PAKISTAN MAKES ABOUT 3 CUPS

1 tablespoon vegetable oil

⅛ teaspoon cumin seeds

¾ cup diced onion

1 tablespoon minced fresh ginger

1 tablespoon minced garlic

1 tablespoon tomato paste

⅛ teaspoon ground turmeric

1 teaspoon garam masala

1 pound ground beef

1 cup peeled, diced white potato

1 cup frozen peas

Salt to taste

Whenever we visit my mother-in-law, she makes *keema* (pronounced "*key*-ma"), also spelled *qeema*, a dish of spiced minced meat with potatoes. The pieces of ground beef are a convenient size for toddlers to handle, and you can adjust the seasonings to make the dish milder or spicier as you wish. This recipe calls for cooking the meat with boiled potato chunks and peas, as is traditional, but you can boil and mash the potato and serve it on the side if you prefer. Round out the meal with fragrant basmati rice.

MAKE In a 3-quart saucepan, heat oil over medium heat. Add cumin seeds and cook until they sputter. Add onions, lower heat, and sauté for 5 minutes, until lightly browned. Add ginger and garlic and cook, stirring continuously, for 1 minute. Add tomato paste, turmeric, and garam masala and cook, stirring constantly, for 3 to 5 minutes, until flavors meld together. Add beef and brown, using a wooden spoon to break up the pieces. When meat is opaque, add potatoes and ¼ cup water and turn heat to medium-low. Cover and cook for 10 to 15 minutes, until beef and potatoes are cooked through and flavors have come together. Add a few more tablespoons of water if mixture appears too dry. In the last few minutes of cooking, add peas.

SERVE Add salt to taste and serve.

Bamya Alicha

ETHIOPIA MAKES ABOUT ¾ CUP

Okra has a reputation for being slimy if poorly cooked. Prepared well, however, okra makes for a nicely spiced toddler finger food, as in *bamya alicha* (pronounced "bam-ee-*yah* ah-*lee*-cha"), a vegetable stew from Ethiopia.

1 teaspoon oil

¼ cup chopped onion

5 large whole okra pods

½ cup no-sodium chicken stock

1 thin slice garlic

1 thin slice fresh ginger

Pinch ground cardamom

Pinch berbere, optional

A WORLD OF FLAVOR:
Berbere

Berbere is a traditional Ethiopian spice blend. Usually made with chilies, fenugreek, ajwain, ginger, garlic, nigella, and other spices, it is spicy, so start with a small quantity and work your way up.

MAKE   In a 2-quart saucepan, heat oil over medium heat. Add onions and sauté, stirring frequently to prevent sticking, for about 3 minutes, or until translucent. Add a bit of water if onions are sticking. Add okra, stock, garlic, ginger, cardamom, and berbere (if using). Cover, turn heat to low, and simmer for about 10 minutes, until okra is soft. Let cool.

SERVE   Remove okra from the pot and slice into bite-size pieces, discarding any particularly large seeds (the seeds are edible, but your baby might not find them palatable).

Jyoti's Goodnight Milk

INDIA MAKES ABOUT 8 OUNCES

1 tablespoon whole almonds

1 tablespoon whole cashews

1 tablespoon shelled pistachios

¼ teaspoon cardamom seeds

⅛ teaspoon ground mace

¼ teaspoon Spanish saffron threads

Pinch freshly grated nutmeg

¼ teaspoon granulated sugar

1 cup whole milk

When I was younger, whenever I couldn't sleep my mom would make me her special version of *thandai*, a popular spiced milk drink from India. She would serve me the blend of warm whole milk, a pinch of sugar, ground cardamom, and a few strands of saffron in a small Mickey Mouse cup, calling it "goodnight milk" and telling me it would make me sleep peacefully and give me happy dreams. I now serve goodnight milk to my four-year-old, who is "never tired," in the same faded cup. I think of my mom each and every time I make it.

PREP In a frying pan over medium-high heat, dry-roast almonds, cashews, and pistachios for 3 to 5 minutes, stirring occasionally, until lightly brown and fragrant. Be careful not to burn nuts. Transfer to a plate and let cool. Place nuts, cardamom, mace, saffron, nutmeg, and sugar in a spice grinder. Grind into a dry powder, being careful not to overgrind; if you go too far, the nuts will start to release moisture and you will end up with a paste. Transfer contents to a glass jar with an airtight lid and store until ready to use. (This is enough spice mixture to flavor 20 cups of milk.)

MAKE Heat milk and 1 teaspoon spice mixture, or more to taste, in a small pan over low heat. You can heat just until warm or boil the milk for a few minutes, which creates a creamier drink.

SERVE Serve warm.

>Variation

Nut-Free Goodnight Milk To 1 cup milk, add a pinch each saffron threads, ground cardamom, and granulated sugar. Heat milk in a small pan over low heat, let cool, and serve.

Atole

MEXICO/GUATEMALA MAKES ABOUT 2 CUPS

½-inch piece vanilla bean pod or ⅛ teaspoon vanilla powder

2½ cups whole milk

¼ cup masa harina

Granulated sugar to taste, optional

⅛ teaspoon ground cinnamon

PREP With a sharp knife, cut vanilla bean pod lengthwise and scrape out seeds with the side of the blade. Use seeds for this recipe, retaining pod for another use.

MAKE In a saucepan, whisk milk and masa harina, making sure there are no lumps. Add sugar (if using), cinnamon, and vanilla seeds and bring to a boil over medium-high heat. Boil for about 4 minutes, until frothy. Keep stirring to avoid lumps and to ensure mixture doesn't boil over.

SERVE Serve warm.

Babies in Mexico are a lucky bunch indeed. *Atole* (pronounced "ah-*toll*-lay") is one of the first beverages (or porridges, depending on how thick you make it) they're able to enjoy. The mixture of milk thickened with masa harina (a special type of corn flour washed with limestone) and seasoned with cinnamon, vanilla, and sugar is boiled until thick and frothy. Make this most comforting, fragrant, and satiating beverage for your little one on a cold, blustery day. Vary the recipe by adding fruit purees (pineapple is very popular) or, for grown-ups, add good-quality chocolate to make a lovely treat called *champurrado*.

Muhallabia

LEBANON MAKES ABOUT 3 CUPS

Muhallabia (pronounced "moo-ha-la-bee-ya") is a traditional Arabic dessert dish, served during celebrations and after long fasts. Children love its flavor and natural sweetness, and it's a nice way to add calcium to your toddler's diet. It is milk seasoned with orange blossom water or rose water, two ingredients typical of Lebanon. I generally avoid adding sugar to baby food, but because muhallabia is an infrequent special dessert, I add a little sugar to it. (You can omit it if you wish.)

¼ cup rice flour

3 cups whole milk, divided

2 tablespoons granulated sugar

2 tablespoons ground almonds

1 teaspoon orange blossom water or rose water

MAKE   In a small bowl, stir rice flour into ½ cup milk. Mix well to avoid lumps. In a 2-quart saucepan, bring the remaining milk and sugar to a boil over medium-high heat. Lower heat to medium and add rice flour mixture and ground almonds. Stir constantly for 5 minutes, until mixture is thick. Add orange blossom or rose water and remove from heat.

SERVE   Let cool enough to drink. Serve warm or transfer mixture to individual serving cups and chill. The pudding will thicken quite a bit as it cools. If your little one prefers a thinner dessert, add more milk to taste.

Known as *purin* in Japanese, *crème caramel* in French, and *flan* in Spanish, caramel custard is a popular dessert in many cultures. I thought I knew everything about this sweet, delicate confection, but then my family and I discovered another spin on the dessert in a Korean bakery near our home. Called "royal pudding," the creamy treat was topped with a layer of fruit puree and then steamed in little glass jars instead of baked.

A WORLD OF FLAVOR:
Vanilla

The rich, sweet taste and gorgeous aroma of vanilla are welcome in many sweet and savory recipes. Different forms of vanilla are available for culinary use: whole beans, extracts, powders, and pastes. When cooking for babies, opt for vanilla powder and vanilla paste, which do not contain alcohol. Make sure to buy "pure" varieties, ones that haven't been adulterated with additives.

Vanilla, Cardamom, and Raspberry Flan

MEXICO/JAPAN/KOREA/CHINA MAKES 2 SERVINGS

Butter for ramekins

1 cup whole milk

1 tablespoon sugar, optional

⅛ teaspoon vanilla powder or pinch of vanilla seeds scraped from pod

Pinch ground cardamom

2 eggs

Raspberry preserves for serving

PREP Butter two ramekins or 6-ounce glass bowls and set aside.

MAKE In a 2-quart saucepan, heat milk, sugar (if using), vanilla powder, and cardamom over medium heat. Do not let mixture boil. In a heat-resistant bowl, gently whisk eggs. Slowly pour warm milk into eggs a little at a time, so eggs do not scramble, and then slowly whisk to prevent air bubbles from forming (this will give the custard a creamier texture).

In a Dutch oven or large pot, heat about 2 cups water over medium heat. (The water should be high enough to come about a quarter of the way up the side of the ramekins when they're placed in the pot.) Pour custard into buttered ramekins and cover each tightly with foil. Carefully place in hot water. Cover pot and simmer, but do not allow to boil, for about 15 minutes, until custard is set. Custard will have a shiny top and wiggle slightly when you tap the side of the ramekin. With tongs, carefully lift ramekins out of pot. Refrigerate for at least 1 hour.

SERVE When ready to serve, spread fruit preserves on top of flan and enjoy.

Gyeran Jjim

KOREA/CHINA MAKES 2 SERVINGS

Butter for ramekins

2 eggs

½ cup low- or no-sodium chicken broth

1 teaspoon chopped scallion

Pinch ground black pepper

Gyeran jjim (pronounced "gee-*ron* gee-jim") is a classic Korean side dish of silky steamed eggs. Your baby will enjoy both the taste and the texture. Transfer eggs to a nonbreakable bowl before serving, or let your toddler eat directly from the ramekin.

MAKE Lightly butter two ramekins. Fill a large pot with about 2 inches of water and place over low heat. The water should come halfway up the side of the ramekins. In a small bowl, whip together eggs, broth, scallions, and pepper. Pour evenly into ramekins. Carefully place ramekins in pot of water. Cover pot and steam eggs on low heat for 12 to 15 minutes, until set. Eggs should be shiny on top and a bit jiggly.

SERVE With tongs, lift ramekins out of pot and let cool. Serve slightly warm.

Masala Egg Scramble

INDIA/PAKISTAN MAKES 1-2 SERVINGS

2 eggs

Splash of whole milk or cream

Pinch garam masala

Butter for pan

Egg spiced with chilies, ginger, garlic, or other seasonings are popular in northern India and Pakistan. My husband's mother always added a pinch of garam masala to eggs when he was a child, and this combination is a hit with our little ones too. Serve it with buttered toast.

MAKE In a small bowl, whisk eggs, milk, and garam masala. Lightly coat a nonstick frying pan with butter and place over medium heat. Add egg mixture and cook, stirring with a spatula, until soft curds form.

SERVE Let cool enough to eat and serve.

Miso Soup

JAPAN MAKES ABOUT 2 CUPS

Miso soup is made with dashi (seaweed stock) and miso (fermented soybean paste). Because it can be quite salty, Japanese parents often serve their baby the *uwa-zumi*, or top portion of the soup (the paste sinks to the bottom of the pot if left to sit). You can reduce the salt by using less miso. The stock base for this soup is made with kelp (a type of seaweed) and bonito flakes; ask your pediatrician about when to serve it to your baby. Japanese babies often start eating miso soup around 6 months old.

1-inch piece dried kelp

¼ cup bonito flakes

1–2 tablespoons organic red miso paste

4 ounces diced tofu, optional

¼ cup sliced scallions, optional

PREP   In a small pot over medium-low heat, bring 2 cups water to a simmer. Add kelp and bonito flakes and simmer for 5 minutes. Strain stock and set liquid aside until ready to make soup; discard solids.

MAKE   Add miso paste, tofu (if using), and scallions (if using) to stock and bring to a simmer over low heat for 2 to 3 minutes. Stir well to break up lumps of miso.

SERVE   Wait a few minutes for soup to settle. Spoon about ½ to 1 inch of the clearer, top portion of broth into a bowl and serve warm. Older babies and adults may eat the rest.

Tamagoyaki

JAPAN MAKES 1 TO 2 SERVINGS

2 large eggs
Dash mirin
Dash soy sauce
Butter for pan

Tamagoyaki (pronounced "ta-ma-go-*yah*-key") is a rolled-up omelet often seasoned with traditional Japanese flavors, such as green onions, garlic, chives, nori, or dashi. It is traditionally cooked in a square pan. A popular component of bento boxes (Japanese portable packed lunches) it is slightly sweet and makes a wonderful food for toddlers.

MAKE In a small bowl, beat eggs, mirin, and soy sauce. Lightly coat a 10-inch nonstick frying pan with butter and heat over medium to high heat. Add egg mixture and swirl so egg covers the entire pan in a thin layer. When egg starts to set, use a spatula to begin rolling it into a log. If egg still looks runny, press roll down and/or flip it to continue cooking the inside of the roll.

SERVE Transfer to a cutting board and cut egg roll into bite-size pieces or slices for finger food.

Sinangag

PHILIPPINES MAKES 1½ CUPS

Garlic for breakfast? Yes! *Sinangag* (pronounced "*sin*-nahn-gahg") is one of the most popular Filipino breakfast and comfort foods. Toasty aromatic garlic oil coats plain white rice, creating a flavorful, savory meal. Add eggs, dried fish, or vegetables to customize the dish. For best results, make sinangag with cold day-old rice.

1 teaspoon vegetable oil

½ garlic clove

1 cup cooked rice, preferably refrigerated overnight

½ cup frozen corn or frozen mixed vegetables

Dash soy sauce

MAKE   In a 2-quart sauté pan or a frying pan, heat oil over medium heat. Mash garlic once with the back of a spoon and add to heated oil. Sauté until just light brown. Add cooked rice and sauté, separating grains as much as possible and coating everything with garlic oil. Add corn, lower heat, cover, and cook for about 2 minutes, until corn is warm. Remove from heat and add soy sauce.

SERVE   Discard garlic clove and serve warm.

A tiny pasta perfect for tiny mouths, pastina is a common first pasta for Italian babies. When cooked, it resembles a porridge, made creamier with butter and Parmesan. Italian mothers often add fresh egg yolk toward the end of cooking (see variation) for more flavor and protein. Season the dish with other flavors as desired: a teaspoon of basil pesto, a sprinkle of salt and pepper, stewed vine-ripened tomatoes (or fresh cherry tomatoes), or diced or pureed vegetables like carrots or eggplant.

Pastina with Parmesan and Nutmeg

ITALY MAKES ABOUT 1 CUP

2 cups water

3 tablespoons pastina

Grated Parmesan cheese, to taste

Pinch grated nutmeg

1 teaspoon butter

MAKE   In a 1-quart saucepan over high heat, bring water to a boil. Add pastina, stir, and return to a boil. Cook uncovered for 6 minutes; taste, and if pasta is not tender enough, cook for an additional minute. Remove from heat, drain, and return pasta to pan. Stir in Parmesan, nutmeg, and butter.

SERVE   Serve warm.

>*Variation*

Pastina with Egg Yolk   In a 1-quart saucepan, bring 1¼ cups water to a boil. Cook pastina as directed above, adding egg yolk in the last minute of cooking. Stir vigorously for 1 to 2 minutes, until yolk is cooked. Remove from heat. Add butter, Parmesan, and nutmeg and continue stirring until a bit of the water has evaporated and the consistency is creamy.

Pasta Romesco

SPAIN/CATALONIA MAKES ABOUT 1 CUP SAUCE

1 red bell pepper

½ cup blanched almonds

½ teaspoon minced garlic

¾ cup chopped tomatoes

1 slice white bread

2 teaspoons olive oil

1 teaspoon Hungarian sweet paprika

4 ounces cooked pasta

Catalonia is a small, autonomous region in northeastern Spain. Catalonians have their own language, sense of identity, and culinary traditions separate and apart from Spain. Romesco is a classic Catalan sauce, often served atop fresh locally caught fish or vegetables. Made with red bell pepper and almonds, it is a nice change of pace from tomato sauce on hot pasta.

MAKE Grasp pepper by the stem with tongs and roast directly over a medium-high flame, turning to blacken all over. Carefully place in a heat-resistant bowl and immediately cover with plastic wrap. Let stand for 15 to 20 minutes. Then use your hands or a wet paper towel to remove all the skin and as much of the charred bits as you can.

Place roasted pepper and remaining ingredients in a mini food processor and blend until smooth.

SERVE Toss with cooked pasta and serve.

A WORLD OF FLAVOR:
Romesco Sauce

Romesco isn't just for pasta. Spread this versatile sauce on bread for a snack, mix it with cooked rice or potatoes, or add as a garnish to meat or vegetable dishes. Blanched almonds are easy to make at home: Soak almonds in boiling water for about 1 minute and then rub off the peels.

For Further Reading

Bentley, Amy. *Inventing Baby Food: Taste, Health, and the Industrialization of the American Diet.* Berkeley: University of California Press, 2014.

Brode, Michelle. "Cultural Aspects of Starting Solids." *New Beginnings* 18, no. 2 (March–April 2001): 64–65.

Cuda-Kroen, Gretchen. "Baby's Palate and Food Memories Shaped Before Birth." *Morning Edition.* NPR. Aug 8, 2011. http://www.npr.org/2011/08/08/139033757/babys-palate-and-food-memories-shaped-before-birth (accessed Dec 17, 2015).

Dewar, Gwen. "Baby Food Secrets: How to Get Babies to Eat New Foods." ParentingScience.com. 2009. http://www.parentingscience.com/baby-food.html (accessed Dec 17, 2015).

———. "Cure for a Picky Eater: Evidence-Based Tips for Getting Kids to Eat Good Foods." Parenting Science.com. 2009–2013. http://www.parentingscience.com/picky-eater.html (accessed Dec 22, 2015).

Fontanel, Béatrice. *Babies Celebrated.* New York: Harry N. Abrams, 1998.

Gibson, R.S., E.L. Ferguson, and J. Lehrfeld. "Complementary Foods for Infant Feeding in Developing Countries: Their Nutrient Adequacy and Improvement." *European Journal of Clinical Nutrition* 52, no. 10 (Oct 1998): 764–70.

Gross-Loh, Christine. *Parenting without Borders, Surprising Lessons Parents around the World Can Teach Us.* New York: Avery, 2013.

Layton, Julia. "How to Develop a Child's Palate." HowStuffWorks.com. July 8, 2009. http://recipes.howstuffworks.com/menus/how-to-develop-a-childs-palate.htm (accessed Dec 22, 2015).

"Maternal, Infant, and Young Child Nutrition in Malawi: Community Nutrition Workers Recipe Book." Dec 2011. http://www.manoffgroup.com/documents/IYCN-Recipes-for-Malawian-children-Dec-2011.pdf (accessed Dec 22, 2015).

Onofiok, N.O., and D.O. Nnanyelugo. "Weaning Foods in West Africa: Nutritional Problems and Possible Solutions." United Nations University Press. n.d. http://archive.unu.edu/unupress/food/V191e/ch06.htm (accessed Dec 22, 2015).

Pak-Gorstein, Suzinne, Aliya Haq, and Elinor A. Graham. "Cultural Influences on Infant Feeding Practices." *Pediatrics in Review* 30, no. 3 (Mar 2009): e11–e21. http://www.pncb.org/ptistore/resource/online_docs/pcc/33-34.pdf (accessed Dec 22, 2015).

Pathak, Dipali. "Early Exposure to Different Flavors Helps Kids Develop Taste for Variety of Foods." Baylor College of Medicine News. Apr 16, 2009.

Rupp, Rebecca. "What's Best for Baby's Tummy? The History of Baby Food." *The Plate*. Dec 29, 2014. http://theplate.nationalgeographic.com/2014/12/29/baby-food/ (accessed Dec 22, 2015).

Swedish National Food Agency. "Good Foods for Infants Under One Year." Sep 2012. http://www.livsmedelsverket.se/globalassets/english/food-habits-health-environment/dietary-guidelines/good-food-for-infants-under-one-year.pdf (accessed Dec 22, 2015).

World Health Organization Department of Nutrition for Health and Development. "Complementary Feeding: Family Foods for Breastfed Children." 2000. http://apps.who.int/iris/bitstream/10665/66389/1/WHO_NHD_00.1.pdf?ua=1&ua=1 (accessed Dec 22, 2015).

Resources

PENZEYS SPICES
Catalog, website, and specialty store chain featuring a huge range of spices.
www.penzeys.com

H MART
Grocery store chain and web store specializing in Asian foods.
www.hmart.com

SAVORY SPICE SHOP
Spice purveyors offering spices, extracts, sauces, and more.
www.savoryspiceshop.com

KALUSTYAN'S
Market specializing in ingredients from India and the Middle East.
123 Lexington Avenue
New York, NY 10016
www.kalustyans.com

PATEL BROTHERS
Grocery store chain featuring Indian foods and spices.
2410 Army Trail Road
Hanover Park, IL 60133
www.patelbros.com

Metric Conversions

Use these rounded equivalents to convert between the traditional American systems used to measure volume and weight and the metric system.

VOLUME

American	Imperial	Metric
$\frac{1}{4}$ tsp		1.25 ml
$\frac{1}{2}$ tsp		2.5 ml
1 tsp		5 ml
$\frac{1}{2}$ tbsp ($1\frac{1}{2}$ tsp)		7.5 ml
1 tbsp (3 tsp)		15 ml
$\frac{1}{4}$ cup (4 tbsp)	2 fl oz	60 ml
$\frac{1}{3}$ cup (5 tbsp)	$2\frac{1}{2}$ fl oz	75 ml
$\frac{1}{2}$ cup (8 tbsp)	4 fl oz	125 ml
$\frac{2}{3}$ cup (10 tbsp)	5 fl oz	150 ml
$\frac{3}{4}$ cup (12 tbsp)	6 fl oz	175 ml
1 cup (16 tbsp)	8 fl oz	250 ml
$1\frac{1}{4}$ cups	10 fl oz	300 ml
$1\frac{1}{2}$ cups	12 fl oz	350 ml
1 pint (2 cups)	16 fl oz	500 ml
$2\frac{1}{2}$ cups	20 fl oz (1 pint)	625 ml
5 cups	40 fl oz (1 qt)	1.25 L

OVEN TEMPERATURES

	°F	°C	Gas Mark
Very cool	250–275	130–140	$\frac{1}{2}$–2
Cool	300	148	2
Warm	325	163	3
Medium	350	177	4
Medium hot	375–400	190–204	5–6
Hot	425	218	7
Very hot	450–475	232–245	8–9

WEIGHTS

American/British	Metric	American/British	Metric
$\frac{1}{4}$ oz	7 g	8 oz ($\frac{1}{2}$ lb)	225 g
$\frac{1}{2}$ oz	15 g	9 oz	250 g
1 oz	30 g	10 oz	280 g
2 oz	55 g	11 oz	310 g
3 oz	85 g	12 oz ($\frac{3}{4}$ lb)	340 g
4 oz ($\frac{1}{4}$ lb)	110 g	13 oz	370 g
5 oz	140 g	14 oz	400 g
6 oz	170 g	15 oz	425 g
7 oz	200 g	16 oz (1 lb)	450 g

Index

Acknowledgments

So often in life you dream of doing what you love, of finding your passion or dream job. The path isn't always straightforward and you question yourself every step of the way. Through writing, cooking, and mothering, I have found a new path and career that I am excited about each and every single day. There are many people to thank for helping me reach this goal.

Without the faith of my agent, Brandi Bowles, I would not be living this dream of becoming a cookbook author. Brandi accepted my book proposal with confidence and enthusiasm. She navigated me through the often-complicated world of publishing and ultimately helped transform me from disgruntled lawyer to happy cookbook author. She believed in me when I didn't believe in myself. Brandi is a smart, savvy, and wonderful agent and I would not be writing these words today without her guidance and friendship.

Brandi brought me to my publisher, Quirk Books. To Tiffany, my editor, and her entire team at Quirk, I cannot thank you enough for making my dreams come true! The first time I met you all I was impressed with your enthusiasm and vision. You are all wonderfully passionate about what you do and I am a very lucky soul to be working with such a talented group of people.

To my sweet little girl Kirina. You are the sole inspiration for this book. If you ate the bland mush I first fed you, we would not be here today. Your love of flavor inspired me to cook for you, to feed you with variety, spices, and love. You led me to this new and wonderful world of cooking, writing, and researching what babies and children eat around the world. Thank you, baby girl. And Ela, my "munches." I thank you for eating everything in this cookbook and doing so with such gusto. You are a sweet and hungry little thing and I love to feed you.

To all the amazing family, friends, and moms all over the world who provided me with inspiration, love, encouragement, and recipes, I thank you from the bottom of my heart. You have been there for me though everything. Two special people I must thank—Sally Bernstein and Jodie Chase. You both gave me such encouragement early on and opportunities to write. You have helped me forge a new career path as a food writer, something I have always dreamed of.

The most important person in this journey has been my best friend and husband, Sunil. You have been steadfast, supportive, loving, and kind beyond words. Thank you for encouraging and believing in me. And for eating whatever I cook. You are the love of my life.

Every time you feed your family, you give them love, life, and nourishment. You also nourish your own soul by providing these comforts. I cook and eat and love because my beloved mom did this for me, and I cannot thank her enough. My mom's memory lives on through every dish, meal, and morsel I feed to my family.